200 Light
slow cooker

hamlyn | all color cookbook

200 Light
slow cooker

An Hachette UK Company
www.hachette.co.uk

First published in Great Britain in 2015 by Hamlyn
a division of Octopus Publishing Group Ltd, Endeavour
House, 189 Shaftesbury Avenue, London, WC2H 8JY
www.octopusbooks.co.uk

Distributed in the US by Hachette Book Group, 1290 Avenue
of the Americas 4th and 5th Floors, New York, NY 10020

Distributed in Canada by Canadian Manda Group,
664 Annette St., Toronto, Ontario, Canada M6S 2C8

ISBN: 978-0-600-62972-6

Printed and bound in China

10 9 8 7 6 5 4 3 2 1

Standard level spoon measurements are used in all recipes.

Ovens should be preheated to the specified temperature
—if using a fan-assisted oven, follow the manufacturer's
instructions for adjusting the time and temperature.

Fresh herbs and medium eggs should be used unless
otherwise stated.

The Food and Drug Administration advises that eggs
should not be consumed raw. This book contains some
dishes made with raw or lightly cooked eggs. It is prudent
for vulnerable people such as pregnant and nusing
mothers, invalids, the elderly, babies, and young children to
avoid uncooked or lightly cooked dishes made with eggs.
Once prepared, these dishes should be kept refrigerated
and used promptly.

This book includes dishes made with nuts and nut
derivatives. It is advisable for those with known allergic
reactions to nuts and nut derivatives and those who may
be potentially vulnerable to these allergies to avoid dishes
made with nuts and nut oils. It is also prudent to check the
labels of pre-prepared ingredients for the possible inclusion
of nut derivatives.

contents

introduction

introduction

this series

The Hamlyn All Color Light Series is a collection of handy-size books, each packed with over 200 healthy recipes on a variety of topics and cuisines to suit your needs.

The books are designed to help those people who are trying to lose weight by offering a range of delicious recipes that are low in calories but still high in flavor. The recipes show a calorie count per portion, so you will know exactly what you are eating. These are recipes for real and delicious food, not ultra-slimming meals, so they will help you maintain a new healthier eating plan for life. They must be used as part of a balanced diet, with the cakes and sweet dishes eaten only as an occasional treat.

how to use this book

All the recipes in this book are clearly marked with the number of calories (kcal) per serving. The chapters cover different calorie bands: under 500, 400, 300, and 200 calories. There are variations on each recipe at the bottom of the page—note the variation calorie counts as they do vary and can sometimes be more than the original recipe.

The figures assume that you are using low-fat versions of dairy products, so be sure to use skim milk and low-fat yogurt. They have also been calculated using lean meat, so make sure you trim meat of all visible fat and remove the skin from chicken breasts.

Use moderate amounts of oil and butter for cooking and low-fat/low-calorie alternatives when you can.

Don't forget to note the number of portions each recipe makes and divide up the food accordingly, so that you know how many calories you are consuming. Be careful about side dishes and accompaniments that will add to calorie content.

Above all, enjoy trying out the new flavors and exciting recipes that this book contains. Rather than dwelling on the thought that you are denying yourself your usual unhealthy treats, think of your new regime as a positive step toward a new you. Not only will you lose weight and feel more confident, but your health will benefit, the condition of your hair and nails will improve, and you will take on a healthy glow.

the risks of obesity

Up to half of women and two-thirds of men are overweight or obese in the developed world today. Being overweight can not only make us unhappy with our appearance, but can also lead to serious health problems.

When someone is obese, it means they are overweight to the point that it could start to seriously threaten their health. In fact, obesity ranks as a close second to smoking as a possible cause of cancer. Obese women are more likely to have complications during and after pregnancy, and people who are overweight or obese are also more likely to have coronary heart disease, gallstones, osteoarthritis, high blood pressure, and type 2 diabetes.

how can I tell if I am overweight?

The best way to tell if you are overweight is to work out your body mass index (BMI). If using metric measurements, divide your weight in kilograms (kg) by your height in meters (m) squared. (For example, if you are 1.7 m tall and weigh 70 kg, the calculation would be 70 ÷ 2.89 = 24.2.) If using imperial measurements, divide your weight in pounds (lb) by your height in inches (in) squared and multiply by 703. Then compare the figure to the list right (these figures apply to healthy adults only).

Less than 20	underweight
20–25	healthy
25–30	overweight
Over 30	obese

As we all know by now, one of the major causes of obesity is eating too many calories.

what is a calorie?

Our bodies need energy to stay alive, grow, keep warm, and be active. We get the energy we need to survive from the food and drinks we consume —more specifically, from the fat, carbohydrate, protein, and alcohol that they contain.

A calorie (cal), as anyone who has ever been on a diet will know, is the unit used to measure how much energy different foods contain. A calorie can be scientifically defined as the energy required to raise the temperature of 1 gram of water from 58.1°F to 59.9°F (14.5°C to 15.5°C). A kilocalorie (kcal) is 1,000 calories and it is, in fact, kilocalories that we usually mean when we talk about the calories in different foods.

Different food types contain different numbers of calories. For example, a gram of carbohydrate (starch or sugar) provides 3.75 kcal, protein provides 4 kcal per gram, fat provides 9 kcal per gram, and alcohol provides 7 kcal per gram. So, fat is the most concentrated source of energy—weight for weight, it provides just over twice as many calories as either protein or carbohydrate

—with alcohol not far behind. The energy content of a food or drink depends on how many grams of carbohydrate, fat, protein, and alcohol are present.

how many calories do we need?

The number of calories we need to consume varies from person to person, but your body weight is a clear indication of whether you are eating the right amount. Body weight is simply determined by the number of calories you are eating compared to the number of calories your body is using to maintain itself and is needed for physical activity. If you regularly consume more calories than you use up, you will start to gain weight as extra energy is stored in the body as fat.

Based on our relatively inactive modern-day lifestyles, most nutritionists recommend that women should aim to consume around 2,000 calories (kcal) per day, and men an amount of around 2,500. Of course, the amount of

energy required depends on your level of activity: the more active you are, the more energy you need to maintain a stable weight.

a healthier lifestyle

To maintain a healthy body weight, we need to expend as much energy as we eat; to lose weight, energy expenditure must therefore exceed intake of calories. So, exercise is a vital tool in the fight to lose weight. Physical activity doesn't just help us control body weight; it also helps to reduce our appetite and is known to have beneficial effects on the heart and blood that help guard against cardiovascular disease.

Many of us claim we don't enjoy exercise and simply don't have the time to fit it into our hectic schedules. So the easiest way to increase physical activity is by incorporating it into our daily routines, perhaps by walking or cycling instead of driving (particularly for short journeys), taking up more active hobbies such as gardening, and taking small and simple steps, such as using the stairs instead of the elevator whenever possible.

As a general guide, adults should aim to undertake at least 30 minutes of moderate-intensity exercise, such as a brisk walk, five times a week. The 30 minutes does not have to be taken all at once: three sessions of 10 minutes are equally beneficial. Children and young people should be encouraged to take at least 60 minutes of moderate-intensity exercise every day.

Some activities will use up more energy than others. The following list shows some examples of the energy a person weighing 132 lb would expend doing the following activities for 30 minutes:

activity	energy
Ironing	69 kcal
Cleaning	75 kcal
Walking	99 kcal
Golf	129 kcal
Fast walking	150 kcal
Cycling	180 kcal
Aerobics	195 kcal
Swimming	195 kcal
Running	300 kcal
Sprinting	405 kcal

make changes for life

The best way to lose weight is to try to adopt healthier eating habits that you can easily maintain all the time, not just when you are trying to slim down. Aim to lose no more than 2 lb per week to ensure you lose only your fat stores. People who go on crash diets lose lean muscle as well as fat and are much more likely to put the weight back on again soon afterward.

For a woman, the aim is to reduce her daily calorie intake to around 1,500 kcal while she is trying to lose weight, then settle on around 2,000 per day thereafter to maintain her new body weight. A regime of regular exercise will also make a huge difference: the more you

can burn, the less you will need to limit your food intake.

improve your diet

For most of us, simply adopting a more balanced diet will reduce our calorie intake and lead to weight loss. Follow these simple recommendations:

- Eat more starchy foods, such as bread, potatoes, rice, and pasta. Assuming these replace the fattier foods you usually eat, and you don't smother them with oil or butter, this will help reduce the amount of fat and increase the amount of fiber in your diet.
- Try to use wholegrain rice, pasta, and flour, as the energy from these foods is released more slowly in the body, making you feel fuller for longer.

- Eat more fruit and vegetables, aiming for at least nine portions of different fruit and vegetables a day (excluding potatoes).
- Eat fewer sugary foods, such as cookies, cakes, and candy bars. This will also help reduce your fat intake. If you fancy something sweet, choose fresh or dried fruit instead.
- Reduce the amount of fat in your diet, so you consume fewer calories. Choosing low-fat versions of dairy products, such as skim milk and low-fat yogurt, doesn't necessarily mean your food will be tasteless. Low-fat versions are available for most dairy products, including milk, cheese, crème fraîche, yogurt, and even cream and butter.
- Choose lean cuts of meat, such as Canadian bacon instead of regular bacon, and chicken breasts instead of thighs. Trim all visible fat off meat before cooking and avoid frying foods—broil or roast them instead. Fish is also naturally low in fat and can make a variety of tempting dishes.

As long as you don't add extra fat to your fruit and vegetables in the form of cream, butter, or oil, these changes will help reduce your fat intake and increase the amount of fiber and vitamins you consume.

simple steps to reduce your intake

Few of us have an iron will, so when you are trying to cut down make it easier on yourself by following these steps:

- Serve small portions to start with. You may feel satisfied when you have finished, but if you are still hungry you can always go back for more.
- Once you have served up your meal, put away any leftover food before you eat. Don't put the serving dishes on the table as you will undoubtedly pick, even if you feel satisfied with what you have already eaten.
- Eat slowly and savor your food; then you are more likely to feel full when you have finished. If you rush a meal, you may still feel hungry afterward.
- Make an effort with your meals. Just because you are cutting down doesn't mean your meals have to be low on taste as well as calories. You will feel more satisfied with a meal you have really enjoyed and will be less likely to look for comfort in a bag of chips or a bar of chocolate.
- Plan your meals in advance to make sure you have all the ingredients you need. Casting around in the pantry when you are hungry is unlikely to result in a healthy, balanced meal.
- Keep healthy and interesting snacks on hand for those moments when you need something to pep you up. You don't need to succumb to a candy bar if there are other tempting, but healthy, treats on offer.

slow cooking

If you want to prepare healthy, homely meals but feel you just don't have time, then think again. As little as 15—20 minutes spent early in the day is all that is needed to prepare supper to go into a slow cooker, leaving you free to get on with something else.

Because the food cooks so slowly there is no need to worry about it boiling dry, spilling over, or burning on the bottom. Depending on the setting it can be left for 8—10 hours. Slow-cooked food often has much more flavor than dishes prepared in other ways.

When water is added to the pot of a slow cooker it can be used as a *bain marie* (water bath) to cook baked custards, pâtés, or terrines. Alcoholic or fruit juice mixtures can be poured into the pot to make warming party punches or hot toddies. Slow cookers are perfect for steaming puddings, too. Because there is no evaporation you won't have to top up the water or return to find that the pot has boiled dry. The slow cooker pot can also be used to make chocolate or cheese fondues, preserves such as lemon curd or simple chutneys, and you can boil up bones or a chicken carcass for homemade stock.

size matters

Unless you have a large family, or like to cook large quantities so that you have enough supper for one meal with extra portions to freeze, you will probably find a slow cooker too big for your everyday needs. Remember that you need to at least half-fill a slow cooker when you are cooking meat, fish, or vegetable dishes.

Slow cookers are available in three sizes and are measured in capacity. The size usually printed on the packaging is the working capacity or the maximum space for food:

- For two people, use a mini oval slow cooker with a maximum capacity of 6 cups (3 pints) and a working capacity of 4 cups (2 pints).

- For four people, choose a round or more versatile oval cooker with a maximum capacity of 3½ quarts and a working capacity of 2½ quarts.

- For six people, you will need a large oval slow cooker with a maximum capacity of 5 quarts and a working capacity of 4 quarts, or an extra large round cooker with a

maximum capacity of 7 quarts and a working capacity of 5 quarts.

The best and most versatile shape for a slow cooker is an oval, which is ideal for cooking a whole chicken and has ample room for a pudding basin or four individual pudding molds and yet is capacious enough to make soup for six. Choose one with an indicator light so that you can see at a glance when the slow cooker is turned on.

before you start

It is important to read the manufacturer's handbook before using your slow cooker. Some recommend preheating the slow cooker on High for a minimum of 20 minutes before food is added. Others recommend that it is heated only when filled with food.

how full should the pot be?

A slow cooker pot must only be used with the addition of liquid—ideally it should be no less than half full. Aim for the three-quarter full mark or, if you are making soups, make sure the liquid is no higher than 1 inch from the top. Joints of meat should take up no more than two-thirds of the pot. If you are using a pudding basin, ensure there is ¾ inch space all the way round or ½ inch at the narrowest point for an oval cooker.

heat settings

All slow cookers have a "high," "low," and "off" setting, and some also have "medium," "warm," or "auto" settings. In general, the "high" setting will take only half the time of the "low" setting when you are cooking a diced meat or vegetable casserole. This can be useful if you plan to eat at lunchtime or are delayed in starting the casserole. Both settings will reach just below 212°F, boiling point, during cooking, but when it is set to 'high' the temperature is reached more quickly. A combination of settings can be useful and is recommended by some manufacturers at the beginning of cooking. (See your manufacturer's handbook for more details.) The following is a general guide to what you should cook at which temperature.

low
• Diced meat or vegetable casseroles
• Chops or chicken joints

- Soups
- Egg custard desserts
- Rice dishes
- Fish dishes

high
- Sweet or savory steamed puddings or sweet dishes that include a leavening agent (either self-rising flour or baking powder)
- Pâtés or terrines
- Whole chicken, guinea fowl, or pheasant, ham joint or half a shoulder of lamb.

timings
All the recipes in this book have variable timings, which means that they will be tender and ready to eat at the shorter time but can be left without spoiling for an extra hour or two, which is perfect if you get delayed at work or stuck in traffic. Do not change timings or slow settings for fish, whole joints, or dairy dishes. If you want to speed up or slow down diced meat or vegetable casseroles, so that the cooking fits around your plans, adjust the heat settings and timings as follows:

Low	Medium	High
6–8 hours	4–6 hours	3–4 hours
8–10 hours	6–8 hours	5–6 hours
10–12 hours	8–10 hours	7–8 hours

(These timings were taken from the Morphy Richards cooker instruction manual.)

Be aware that as the slow cooker heats up, it forms a water seal just under the lid, but whenever you lift the lid you break the seal. For each time you lift the lid, add 20 minutes to the cooking time. Any precooking is included in the prepararion time.

using your slow cooker for the first time
- Before you start to use the slow cooker, put it on the work surface, somewhere out of the way and make sure that the flex is tucked around the back of the machine and not trailing over the front of the work surface.
- The outside of the slow cooker does get hot, so warn young members of the family.
- Don't forget to wear oven mitts or use dish towels when you are lifting the pot out of the housing, and always place the pot on

a heatproof mat on the table or work surface to serve the food.

- Don't put your slow cooker under an eye-level cabinet if the lid has a vent in the top. The steam from the vent could burn someone's arm as they reach into the cabinet.

- Always check that the joint, pudding basin, soufflé dish, or individual molds will fit into your slow cooker pot before you begin work on a recipe to avoid frustration when you get to a critical point.

preparing food for the slow cooker

Meat: Cut meat into pieces that are the same size so cooking is even, and fry off meat before adding to the slow cooker. A whole guinea fowl or pheasant, a small ham joint or half a shoulder of lamb can be cooked in an oval slow cooker pot, but make sure that it does not fill more than the lower two-thirds of the pot. Cover the meat with boiling liquid and cook on high. Check it is cooked either by using a meat thermometer or by inserting the tip of a sharp knife through the thickest part and ensuring that the juices run clear. Add boiling stock or sauce to the slow cooker pot and press the meat beneath the surface before cooking begins.

Vegetables: Root vegetables can (surprisingly) take longer to cook than meat. If you are adding vegetables to a meat casserole, make sure you cut them into pieces that are a little

smaller than the meat and try to keep all the vegetable chunks the same size so that they cook evenly. Press the vegetables and the meat below the surface of the liquid before cooking begins. When you are making soup, puree it while it is still in the slow cooker pot, using an electric immersion blender if you have one.

Fish: Whether you cut the fish into pieces or cook it in a larger piece of about 1 lb, the slow, gentle cooking will not cause the fish to break up or overcook. Always make sure that the fish is covered by the hot liquid so that it cooks evenly right through to the center and do not add shellfish until the last 15 minutes of cooking, when the slow cooker should be set to high. Any frozen fish must be thoroughly thawed, rinsed with cold water, and drained before use.

Pasta: For best results, cook the pasta separately in a saucepan of boiling water and then mix with the casserole just before serving. Small pasta shapes, such as macaroni or shells, can be added to soups 30–45 minutes before the end of cooking. Pasta can be soaked in boiling water for 10 minutes prior to adding to short-cook recipes.

Rice: Easy-cook rice is preferable for slow cookers because it has been partially cooked during manufacture and some of the starch has been washed off, making it less sticky. When you are cooking rice, allow a minimum of 1 cup water for each ½ cup of easy-cook rice, or up to 2 cups for risotto rice.

Dried legumes: Make sure that you soak dried legumes in plenty of cold water overnight. Drain them, then put them into a saucepan with fresh water and bring to a boil. Boil rapidly for 10 minutes, skim off any foam, then drain or add with the cooking liquid to the slow cooker. (See recipes for details.)

changing recipes to suit a different model

All the recipes in this book have been tested in a standard-size slow cooker for four people with a maximum capacity of 3½ quarts. You might have a larger 5 quart six-portion size cooker or a smaller 3 pint two-portion cooker. To adapt the recipes in this book you can simply halve for two portions or add half as much again to the recipe for more portions, keeping the timings the same. All those recipes made in a pudding basin, soufflé dish, or individual molds may also be cooked in a larger slow cooker for the same amount of time.

caring for your slow cooker

If you look after it carefully you may find that your machine lasts for 20 years or more.

Because the heat of a slow cooker is so controllable it is not like a saucepan with burned-on grime to contend with. Once cool, simply lift the slow cooker pot out of the housing, fill the pot with hot, soapy water and let soak for a while. Although it is tempting to pop the slow cooker pot and lid into the dishwasher, they do take up a lot of space and not all are dishwasher proof (check your manual).

Allow the machine itself to cool down before cleaning. Turn it off at the controls and pull out the plug. Wipe the inside with a damp cloth, removing any stubborn marks with a little cream cleaner. The outside of the machine and the controls can be wiped with a cloth, then buffed up with a duster or, if it has a chrome-effect finish, sprayed with a little multisurface cleaner and polished with a duster. Never immerse the machine in water to clean it and if you are storing the slow cooker in a cabinet, make sure it is completely cold before you put it away.

recipes under 200 calories

breakfast baked tomatoes

Calories per serving **121**
Serves **4**
Preparation time **10 minutes**
Cooking time **8–10 hours**

1 lb **plum tomatoes**, halved
    lengthwise
leaves from 2–3 **thyme sprigs**
1 tablespoon **balsamic
    vinegar**
salt and **pepper**
chopped **parsley**, to garnish
4 slices of **whole-wheat
    bread**, 1½ oz each, to serve

Preheat the slow cooker if necessary. Arrange the tomatoes, cut sides up, in the slow cooker pot, packing them in tightly in a single layer. Sprinkle with the thyme, drizzle with the vinegar, and season with salt and pepper to taste. Cover and cook on Low for 8–10 hours overnight.

Toast the bread the next morning and place on 4 serving plates. Top with the tomatoes and a little of the juice and serve sprinkled with parsley.

For balsamic tomatoes with spaghetti, follow the recipe above to cook the tomatoes, then chop them and mix with the cooking juices. Cook 7 oz dried spaghetti according to package instructions, then drain and toss with the tomatoes. Sprinkle each portion with 1 tablespoon grated Parmesan cheese.
Calories per serving 242

tomato, pepper & garlic bruschetta

Calories per serving **197**
Serves **4**
Preparation time **20 minutes**
Cooking time **3–5 hours**

1 large **red bell pepper**,
  quartered, cored, and
  seeded
1 lb **plum tomatoes**, halved
4 large **garlic cloves**,
  unpeeled
leaves from 2–3 **thyme sprigs**
1 teaspoon **granular**
  sweetener
1 tablespoon **virgin olive oil**
8 slices of **French bread**,
  6 oz in total
8 **pitted black ripe olives**
  in brine, drained
salt and **pepper**

Preheat the slow cooker if necessary. Arrange the pepper pieces, skin side down, in the bottom of the slow cooker pot, arrange the tomatoes on top, then tuck the garlic in among them. Sprinkle the thyme leaves on top, reserving a little to garnish. Sprinkle with the sweetener and drizzle with the oil.

Season with salt and pepper to taste, cover, and cook on High for 3–5 hours, until the vegetables are tender but the tomatoes still hold their shape.

Lift the vegetables out of the slow cooker pot with a slotted spoon. Peel the skins off the peppers, tomatoes, and garlic, then coarsely chop the vegetables and toss together. Adjust the seasoning if necessary.

Toast the bread on both sides, arrange on a serving plate, then spoon the tomato mixture on top. Arrange the olives and reserved thyme on the bruschetta and serve as a light lunch or appetizer.

For quick tomato & pepper pizzas, follow the recipe above to cook the tomato and pepper mixture, then spoon onto 2 halved and toasted ciabatta rolls. Sprinkle with ½ cup shredded reduced-fat cheddar cheese and place under a preheated hot broiler to melt the cheese. Serve with salad. **Calories per serving 237**

baked peppers with chorizo

Calories per serving **105**
Serves **4**
Preparation time **20 minutes**
Cooking time **3–4 hours**

2 large **red bell peppers**,
  halved lengthwise, cored,
  and seeded
2 **scallions**, thinly sliced
2 oz **chorizo**, finely diced
1 cup **cherry tomatoes**,
  halved
1–2 **garlic cloves**, finely
  chopped
small handful of **basil**, torn,
  plus extra to garnish
4 pinches of **smoked hot
  paprika**
1 tablespoon **balsamic
  vinegar**
salt and **pepper**

Preheat the slow cooker if necessary. Arrange the peppers, cut sides up, in a single layer in the bottom of the slow cooker pot. Divide the scallions and chorizo among the peppers, then pack in the cherry tomatoes.

Sprinkle with the garlic and torn basil, then add a pinch of paprika and a drizzle of balsamic vinegar to each one. Season with salt and pepper to taste, cover, and cook on High for 3–4 hours, until the peppers have softened.

Transfer to a plate and sprinkle with extra basil leaves. Serve hot or cold as a light lunch with salad.

For baked pepper pizzas, follow the recipe above, omitting the chorizo and paprika. When cooked, transfer the peppers to a shallow ovenproof dish. Tear 5 oz mozzarella into small pieces, sprinkle over the peppers, then place under a preheated hot broiler for 4–5 minutes, until the cheese is bubbling and golden. Garnish with extra torn basil and 4 pitted black ripe olives. **Calories per serving 155**

herby stuffed peppers

Calories per serving **190**
Preparation time **20 minutes**
Cooking time **4—5 hours**
Serves **4**

4 **different colored bell**
  peppers
½ cup easy-cook **brown rice**
15 oz can **chickpeas**, drained
small bunch of **parsley**,
  coarsely chopped
small bunch of **mint**, coarsely
  chopped
1 **onion**, finely chopped
2 **garlic cloves**, finely chopped
½ teaspoon **smoked paprika**
1 teaspoon **ground allspice**
2½ cups hot **vegetable stock**
salt and **pepper**

Preheat the slow cooker if necessary. Cut the top off
each pepper, then remove the core and seeds.

Mix together the rice, chickpeas, herbs, onion, garlic,
paprika, and allspice with plenty of seasoning. Spoon
the mixture into the insides of the peppers, then put the
peppers into the slow cooker pot.

Pour the hot stock around the peppers, cover with the
lid, and cook on Low for 4—5 hours or until the rice and
peppers are tender. Spoon into dishes and serve.

For feta-stuffed peppers, make the recipe as above,
but use 3½ oz crumbled feta cheese, ¼ cup golden
raisins, a small bunch of chopped basil, and ¼ teaspoon
ground allspice instead of the chopped parsley, mint,
paprika, and allspice. **Calories per serving 213**

indian black pepper chicken

Calories per serving **194**
Serves **4**
Preparation time **20 minutes**
Cooking time **7½–8¾ hours**

1 large **onion**, quartered
3 **garlic cloves**, halved
1½ inch piece of **fresh ginger root**, sliced
1 cup **fresh cilantro**
8 small skinless **chicken drumsticks**, 1¾ lb in total
low-calorie cooking oil spray
2 inch **cinnamon stick**
1 teaspoon **ground cumin**
1 teaspoon **ground turmeric**
2 teaspoons **black peppercorns**, coarsely crushed
juice of ½ **lemon**
1½ cups **chicken stock**
3 cups **baby spinach**
salt

Preheat the slow cooker if necessary. Place the onion, garlic, ginger, and cilantro in a food processor and blitz until very finely chopped.

Slash each chicken drumstick 2 or 3 times with a sharp knife. Spray a large skillet with a little low-calorie cooking oil spray and place over high heat until hot. Add the chicken and cook for 4–5 minutes, turning until browned all over. Transfer to the slow cooker pot, packing them in tightly together.

Add the chopped onion mixture to the skillet and cook for 2 minutes, until just softened. Stir in the cinnamon, cumin, turmeric, and peppercorns, then add the lemon juice and stock. Season with salt to taste and bring to a boil, stirring.

Pour the hot stock over the chicken, cover, and cook on Low for 7–8 hours, until the chicken is cooked through and beginning to shrink on the bones. Stir the sauce, add the spinach, cover again, and cook on High for 15–30 minutes, until the spinach has wilted. Spoon into shallow bowls and serve immediately.

For Indian chicken & chickpea curry, follow the recipe above, using just 4 chicken drumsticks and adding ¼ teaspoon chili powder instead of the black pepper. Place the browned drumsticks in the slow cooker pot with a 15 oz can of chickpeas, drained, then pour over the hot stock and cook as above. **Calories per serving 123**

slow-cooked ratatouille

Calories per serving **135**
Serves **4**
Preparation time **20 minutes**
Cooking time **3¾–5 hours**

low-calorie cooking oil spray
1 **onion**, chopped
1 large **eggplant**, halved
   lengthwise and sliced
2 **garlic cloves**, finely chopped
1 **red bell pepper**, cored,
   seeded, and diced
1 **orange bell pepper**, cored,
   seeded, and diced
14½ oz can **diced tomatoes**
⅔ cup **vegetable stock**
1 teaspoon **granular**
   sweetener
1 teaspoon **dried**
   Mediterranean herbs
2 teaspoons **cornstarch**
1 lb **zucchini**, thickly sliced
1 cup **cherry tomatoes**,
   halved
salt and **pepper**
small handful of **basil leaves**,
   to garnish

Preheat the slow cooker if necessary. Spray a large skillet with a little low-calorie cooking oil spray and place over high heat until hot. Add the onion and eggplant and cook for 5 minutes, until just beginning to brown.

Stir in the garlic, peppers, tomatoes, stock, sweetener, and dried herbs, season to taste, then bring to a boil, stirring. Transfer to the slow cooker pot, cover, and cook on High for 3–4 hours, until the vegetables are tender.

Mix the cornstarch to a smooth paste with a little cold water and stir into the pot with the zucchini and cherry tomatoes. Cover again and cook for 30–45 minutes, until the zucchini are just tender. Garnish with basil and serve.

For ribollita, the Italian version of ratatouille, follow the recipe above, omitting the eggplant and adding a 15 oz can of navy beans, drained, to the skillet with the stock. Cook as above, then stir in 2½ cups spinach leaves for the final 15 minutes of cooking. **Calories per serving 194**

thai broth with fish dumplings

Calories per serving **189**
Serves **4**
Preparation time **30 minutes**
Cooking time 2¼–3¼ **hours**

3¾ cups boiling **fish stock**
2 teaspoons **Thai fish sauce**
 (nam pla)
1 tablespoon **Thai red curry**
 paste
1 tablespoon **soy sauce**
½ bunch of **scallions**, sliced
1 **carrot**, thinly sliced
2 **garlic cloves**, finely chopped
1 bunch of **asparagus**,
 trimmed and stems cut
 into 4
2 **bok choy**, thickly sliced

Dumplings
½ bunch of **scallions**, sliced
1 cup **cilantro leaves**
1½ inches **fresh ginger root**,
 peeled and sliced
13 oz **cod**, skinned
1 tablespoon **cornstarch**
1 **egg white**

Preheat the slow cooker if necessary. Make the dumplings. Put the scallions into a food processor with the cilantro and ginger and chop finely. Add the cod, cornstarch, and egg white and process until the fish is finely chopped. With wetted hands, shape the mixture into 12 balls.

Pour the boiling fish stock into the slow cooker pot, add the fish sauce, curry paste, and soy sauce. Add the scallions, the carrot, and garlic and drop in the dumplings. Cover with the lid and cook on Low for 2–3 hours.

When almost ready to serve, add the asparagus and bok choy to the broth. Replace the lid and cook on High for 15 minutes or until just tender. Ladle into bowls and serve.

For Thai broth with noodles & shrimp, prepare and cook the broth as above, omitting the dumplings, for 2–3 hours. Add the asparagus, bok choy, and 7 oz frozen large shrimp, thoroughly thawed, and cook for 15 minutes on High. Meanwhile, soak 3 oz rice noodles in boiling water according to the package instructions. Drain and add to the bottom of 4 soup bowls. Ladle the broth on top and sprinkle with a little chopped cilantro. **Calories per serving 185**

spinach & zucchini tian

Calories per serving **180**
Serves **4**
Preparation time **20 minutes**
Cooking time **1¾–2¼ hours**

¼ cup **long-grain rice**
1 tablespoon **olive oil**, plus
  extra for greasing
1 **tomato**, sliced
½ **onion**, chopped
1 **garlic clove**, finely chopped
1 cup coarsely shredded
  zucchini
2½ cups **spinach**, thickly
  shredded
3 **eggs**
6 tablespoons **milk**
pinch of grated **nutmeg**
¼ cup chopped **mint**
salt and **pepper**

Preheat the slow cooker if necessary. Cook the rice in a saucepan of lightly salted boiling water according to package instructions until tender.

Meanwhile, grease the bottom and sides of a 5½ inch round ovenproof dish, about 3½ inches deep, with a little oil and line the bottom with nonstick parchment paper. Arrange the tomato slices, overlapping, in the bottom of the dish.

Heat the oil in a skillet over medium heat, add the onion and cook for 5 minutes, until softened. Stir in the garlic, zucchini, and spinach and cook for 2 minutes or until the spinach has just wilted.

Beat together the eggs, milk, and nutmeg and season with salt and pepper to taste. Drain the rice and stir into the spinach mixture with the egg mixture and mint. Mix well, then spoon into the dish. Cover loosely with greased foil and place in the slow cooker pot.

Pour boiling water into the slow cooker pot to come halfway up the sides of the dish, cover, and cook on High for 1½–2 hours or until the tian is set in the middle. Remove from the slow cooker, let stand for 5 minutes, then remove the foil, loosen the edges, and turn out onto a plate. Cut into wedges and serve warm with salad, if desired.

For cheesy spinach & pine nut tian, follow the recipe above, omitting the zucchini and stirring ½ cup freshly grated Parmesan cheese, a small bunch of chopped basil, and ¼ cup toasted pine nuts into the mixture instead of the mint. **Calories per serving 299**

chicken noodle broth

Calories per serving **133**
Serves **4**
Preparation time **10 minutes**
Cooking time **5 hours 20**
  minutes–7½ hours

1 **chicken carcass**
1 **onion**, cut into wedges
2 **carrots**, sliced
2 **celery sticks**, sliced
1 **bouquet garni**
5 cups **boiling water**
3 oz **vermicelli pasta**
¼ cup chopped **parsley**
salt and **pepper**

Preheat the slow cooker if necessary. Place the chicken carcass in the slow cooker pot, breaking it into 2 pieces if necessary to make it fit. Add the onion, carrots, celery, and bouquet garni. Pour over the boiling water and season with salt and pepper to taste. Cover and cook on High for 5–7 hours.

Strain the soup through a large strainer, then return the liquid to the slow cooker pot. Remove any meat from the carcass and add to the pot. Adjust the seasoning if necessary, add the pasta and cook for another 20–30 minutes, until the pasta is just cooked. Sprinkle with the parsley, ladle into deep bowls, and serve.

For chicken & minted pea soup, follow the recipe above to make the soup, then strain and pour it back into the slow cooker pot. Add 1 cup finely sliced leeks, 2½ cups frozen peas, and a small bunch of mint, cover, and cook for another 30 minutes. Puree the soup in a blender or with a hand-held immersion blender, then stir in ⅔ cup mascarpone cheese until melted. Ladle into bowls and sprinkle with extra mint, if desired.
Calories per serving 255

roasted vegetable terrine

Calories per serving **199**
Serves **4**
Preparation time **20 minutes,
    plus cooling**
Cooking time **2¼–3¼ hours**

2½ cups thinly sliced **zucchini**
1 **red bell pepper**, cored,
    seeded, and quartered
1 **orange bell pepper**, cored,
    seeded, and quartered
2 tablespoons **olive oil**, plus
    extra for greasing
1 **garlic clove**, finely chopped
2 **eggs**
⅔ cup **milk**
¼ cup grated **Parmesan
    cheese**
3 tablespoons chopped **basil**
salt and **pepper**

Preheat the slow cooker if necessary. Line a broiler rack with foil and arrange all the vegetables on it in a single layer, with the peppers skin sides up. Drizzle with the oil, sprinkle with the garlic, and season with salt and pepper. Broil for 10 minutes or until softened and golden. Transfer the zucchini slices to a plate and wrap the peppers in the foil. Let stand for 5 minutes to loosen the skins.

Oil a 1 lb loaf pan and line the bottom and two long sides with nonstick parchment paper, checking first it will fit in the slow cooker pot. Beat together the eggs, milk, Parmesan, and basil in a bowl and season to taste. Unwrap the peppers and peel away the skins.

Arrange one-third of the zucchini slices over the bottom and sides of the pan. Spoon in a little custard, then add half the peppers in a single layer and a little more custard. Repeat, ending with a layer of zucchini and custard. Cover the top with foil and put in the slow cooker pot.

Pour boiling water into the pot to come halfway up the sides of the pan, cover, and cook on High for 2–3 hours or until the custard has set. Remove the tin from the slow cooker and let cool.

Loosen the edges of the terrine with a round-bladed knife, turn out onto a plate and peel off the lining paper. Cut into slices and serve with romesco sauce, if desired.

For romesco sauce, to serve as an accompaniment, cook 1 chopped onion in 1 tablespoon olive oil in a skillet for 5 minutes, until softened. Add 2 chopped garlic cloves, 4 skinned and chopped tomatoes, ½ teaspoon paprika and ½ cup finely chopped almonds. Simmer for 10 minutes until thick, season to taste, and let cool. **Calories per serving 125**

baked honey & orange custards

Calories per serving **144**
Serves **4**
Preparation time **15 minutes,
plus cooling and chilling**
Cooking time **4–5 hours**

2 **eggs**
2 **egg yolks**
1²⁄₃ cups **low-fat milk**
1 tablespoon **granular
sweetener**
1 tablespoon **runny honey**
½ teaspoon **vanilla extract**
finely grated zest of ½ **orange,**
plus extra to garnish
large pinch of **ground
cinnamon**

Preheat the slow cooker if necessary. Place the eggs, egg yolks, and milk in a mixing bowl with the sweetener, honey, and vanilla and whisk together until smooth. Strain the mixture through a sieve into a large pitcher, then whisk in the orange zest.

Divide the mixture among 4 x ²⁄₃ cup ovenproof dishes (checking first that the dishes fit in your slow cooker pot). Place the dishes in the slow cooker pot and sprinkle the cinnamon over the top. Pour hot water into the slow cooker pot until it comes halfway up the sides of the dishes. Cover the tops of the dishes with foil, place the lid on the slow cooker, and cook on Low for 4–5 hours, until set.

Remove the dishes from the slow cooker and let cool. Transfer to the refrigerator to chill well before serving, garnished with a little extra orange zest.

For vanilla crème brûlée, follow the recipe above to cook and chill the custards, using 1 teaspoon vanilla extract and omitting the orange zest and cinnamon. Just before serving, sprinkle 1 teaspoon sugar over the top of each dish and caramelize the sugar with a cook's blow torch or under a preheated hot broiler. Cool for a few minutes to allow the sugar to set hard, then serve with a few fresh raspberries. **Calories per serving 193**

baked apples with blackberries

Calories per serving **95**
Serves **4**
Preparation time **15 minutes**
Cooking time **3–3½ hours**

4 **Gala dessert apples**,
   14 oz in total
1 cup **blackberries**
1 tablespoon **blackberry**
   or **blueberry jelly**
6 tablespoons **pressed apple**
   juice

Preheat the slow cooker if necessary. Use an apple corer or small knife to remove the cores from the apples, then enlarge the holes slightly at the top and place the apples in the slow cooker pot.

Press a few of the blackberries into the apple cavities, then dot with jelly. Push the remaining berries into the cavities, then pour the apple juice into the slow cooker pot. Cover and cook on High for 3–3½ hours, until the apples are soft but still a bright color.

Serve in shallow bowls with some of the juice spooned over.

For Christmas baked apples, core the apples as above and place in the slow cooker pot. Mix 4 teaspoons Christmas mincemeat with a large pinch of ground cinnamon and ¼ cup ready-to-eat dried apricots, diced. Use the mixture to fill the apples, pour 6 tablespoons apple juice into the slow cooker pot, and cook as above. **Calories per serving 119**

apricot & cardamom fool

Calories per serving **126**
Serves **4**
Preparation time **15 minutes,
plus cooling and chilling**
Cooking time **1½–2 hours**

11 oz **apricots**, halved, pitted,
and cut into chunks
2 **cardamom pods**, crushed
1 tablespoon **honey**
¼ cup **water**
⅔ cup **prepared custard**
⅔ cup **fromage frais** or **low-
fat plain yogurt**

Preheat the slow cooker if necessary. Place the apricots in the slow cooker pot with the crushed cardamom pods and their black seeds. Drizzle over the honey and water, cover, and cook on Low for 1½–2 hours, until the apricots are soft.

Remove the pot from the slow cooker and let cool for 30 minutes. Discard the cardamom pods and puree the fruit in a blender or with a hand-held immersion blender.

Mix the custard with the fromage frais and place a spoonful in each of 4 serving glasses. Add a spoonful of the fruit mixture and continue alternating custard and fruit to fill the glasses. Swirl the ingredients together with the handle of a teaspoon and chill until ready to serve.

For plum & cinnamon fool, place 11 oz chopped ripe red plums in the slow cooker pot with ½ teaspoon ground cinnamon, 1 tablespoon honey, and ¼ cup water. Cook as above, allow to cool, then puree. Swirl with the custard and fromage frais, chill, and serve as for the main recipe. **Calories per serving 131**

baked peaches with ginger

Calories per serving **105**
Serves **4**
Preparation time **10 minutes**
Cooking time **1½–2½ hours**

1 inch piece of **fresh ginger
    root**, finely chopped
6 ripe **peaches**, halved and
    pitted
6 tablespoons **pressed apple
    juice**
1 tablespoon **sugar**
¾ cup **blueberries**
⅔ cup **0% fat Greek yogurt**

Preheat the slow cooker if necessary. Arrange the chopped ginger over the bottom of the slow cooker pot, then place the peaches, cut sides down, on top in a single layer. Pour over the apple juice, then sprinkle with the sugar and blueberries.

Cover and cook on Low for 1½–2½ hours, until the peaches are piping hot and the juices are beginning to run from the blueberries. Spoon into serving bowls and serve warm or cold with the Greek yogurt.

For baked peaches with rosé wine, arrange 8 peach halves, cut sides down, in the bottom of the slow cooker pot and pour over 6 tablespoons rosé wine, 1 tablespoon sugar, and 1 cup raspberries instead of the blueberries. Cover, cook and serve as above. **Calories per serving 100**

plum & blueberry swirl

Calories per serving **110**
Serves **4**
Preparation time **15 minutes**
Cooking time **2¼–2¾ hours**

10 oz ripe **red plums**, halved,
   pitted, and cut into chunks
1¼ cups **blueberries**
1 tablespoon **granular**
   sweetener
juice of ½ **orange**
3 tablespoons **water**
1 tablespoon **cornstarch**

Yogurt
¾ cup **0% fat Greek yogurt**
finely grated zest of ½ **orange**
1 tablespoon **granular**
   sweetener

Preheat the slow cooker if necessary. Place the plums and blueberries in the slow cooker pot, sprinkle with the sweetener, then add the orange juice and water. Cover and cook on High for 2–2½ hours, until the fruit is soft.

Mix the cornstarch to a smooth paste with a little cold water and stir into the pot. Cover again and cook for another 15 minutes until thickened, stir the fruit and let cool.

Mix the yogurt with the orange zest and sweetener. Divide the fruit among 4 serving glasses, top with the yogurt, then swirl together with a teaspoon. Chill until ready to serve.

For minted strawberry & blueberry swirl, place 2 cups ripe strawberries in the slow cooker pot with 1¼ cups blueberries, 1 tablespoon sweetener, and the juice of ½ orange. Cook as above, then thicken with the cornstarch, cook for a further 15 minutes, and let cool. Mix ¾ cup 0% fat Greek yogurt with 1 tablespoon chopped mint and 1 tablespoon granular sweetener, then swirl with the fruit as above. **Calories per serving 102**

spiced pears

Calories per serving **83**
Serves **4**
Preparation time **15 minutes**
Cooking time **3–4 hours**

1 ¼ cups **hot water**
4 **cardamom pods**, crushed
3 inch **cinnamon stick**, halved
1 inch piece of **fresh ginger
    root**, thinly sliced
2 teaspoons **granular
    sweetener**
4 **pears** with stalks, peeled,
    halved lengthwise, and cored
pared peel and juice of
    1 **lemon**
pared peel and juice of
    1 **orange**

Preheat the slow cooker if necessary. Pour the hot water into the slow cooker pot, then stir in the cardamom pods and their black seeds, the cinnamon, ginger, and sweetener.

Add the pears and the lemon and orange juice, then gently turn the pears in the liquid to coat and arrange them cut sides down in a single layer. Cut the pared lemon and orange peel into very thin strips and sprinkle on top.

Cover and cook on Low for 3–4 hours, until the pears are tender. The cooking time will depend on their ripeness. Serve warm.

For mulled wine pears, follow the recipe above, using ⅔ cup red wine and ⅔ cup hot water instead of 1 ¼ cups hot water, and using 4 cloves instead of the cardamom pods. Increase the sweetener to 1 tablespoon, or to taste, and cook as above. **Calories per serving 99**

recipes under 300 calories

vanilla breakfast prunes & figs

Calories per serving **299**
Serves **4**
Preparation time **5 minutes**
Cooking time **8—10 hours** or
   overnight

1 **breakfast tea** teabag
2½ cups boiling **water**
1 cup pitted **prunes**
1 cup dried **figs**
⅓ cup **sugar**
1 teaspoon **vanilla extract**
zest of ½ **orange**

To serve
plain yogurt
granola

Preheat the slow cooker if necessary. Put the teabag into a pitcher or teapot, add the boiling water and let to soak for 2–3 minutes. Remove the teabag and pour the tea into the slow cooker pot.

Add the whole prunes and figs, the sugar, and vanilla extract to the hot tea, sprinkle with the orange zest and mix together. Cover with the lid and cook on low for 8–10 hours or overnight.

Serve hot with spoonfuls of plain yogurt and a sprinkling of granola.

For breakfast apricots in orange, put 2 cups dried apricots, ¼ cup sugar, 1¼ cups boiling water, and ⅔ cup orange juice in the slow cooker pot. Cover and cook as above. **Calories per serving 295**

brunch poached eggs & haddock

Calories per serving **247**

Serves **2**

Preparation time **5 minutes**

Cooking time **1–1¼ hours**

low-calorie cooking oil spray

2 **eggs**

1 teaspoon chopped **chives**

2 **smoked haddock steaks**,
   4 oz each

2 cups boiling **water**

2½ cups **baby spinach**

1 tablespoon **butter**

salt and **pepper**

Preheat the slow cooker if necessary. Spray the insides of 2 small ovenproof dishes or ramekins with a little low-calorie cooking oil spray, then break an egg into each. Sprinkle with a few chives and season with salt and pepper to taste.

Place the egg dishes in the center of the slow cooker pot, then arrange a fish steak on each side. Pour the boiling water over the fish so that the water comes halfway up the sides of the dishes. Cover and cook on High for 1–1¼ hours, until the eggs are done to your liking and the fish flakes easily when pressed with a small knife.

Rinse the spinach with a little water, drain and place in a microwave-proof dish. Cover and cook in a microwave on full power for 1 minute, until just wilted. Divide between 2 serving plates, and top with the fish steaks. Loosen the eggs with a knife and turn out of their dishes on top of the fish. Sprinkle with chopped chives, season with salt and pepper, and serve.

For brunch poached eggs with salmon, follow the recipe above, using 2 wild salmon steaks, 3½ oz each, instead of the smoked haddock. Arrange 2 sliced tomatoes on the serving plates, top with the cooked salmon and eggs and serve. **Calories per serving 291**

baked eggs with toast

Calories per serving **295**
Serves **4**
Preparation time **15 minutes**
Cooking time **40–50 minutes**

2 tablespoons **butter**
4 thin slices of **honey roast
   ham**, 2½ oz in total
4 teaspoons **spicy tomato
   chutney**
4 **eggs**
2 **cherry tomatoes**, halved
1 **scallion**, finely sliced
salt and **pepper**
4 slices of thinly spread
   buttered **toast**, to serve

Preheat the slow cooker if necessary. Use a little of the butter to grease ⅔ cup ovenproof dishes (checking first that the dishes fit in your slow cooker pot). Press a slice of ham into each dish to line the bottom and sides, leaving a small overhang of ham above the dish.

Place 1 teaspoon of chutney in the bottom of each dish, then break an egg on top. Add a cherry tomato half to each, sprinkle with the scallion, season to taste, then dot with the remaining butter. Cover the tops with greased foil and put in the slow cooker pot.

Pour boiling water into the slow cooker pot to come halfway up the sides of the dishes, cover, and cook on High for 40–50 minutes or until the egg whites are set and the yolks still slightly soft.

Remove the foil and gently run a round-bladed knife between the ham and the edges of the dishes. Turn out and quickly turn the baked eggs the right way up. Place each on a plate and serve with the hot buttered toast, cut into fingers.

For eggs Benedict, butter 4 dishes as above, then break an egg into each. Season to taste, sprinkle the eggs with 1 sliced scallion and dot with 2 tablespoons butter. Cover and cook as above. To serve, broil 8 Canadian bacon slices until golden. Toast 4 halved English breakfast muffins, spread with butter, divide the bacon among the lower halves and arrange on serving plates. Top with the baked eggs and drizzle with ¼ cup warmed prepared hollandaise sauce. Replace the muffin tops and serve immediately.
Calories per serving 492

hearty winter sausage stew

Calories per serving **299**
Serves **4**
Preparation time **20 minutes**
Cooking time **5¼–6¼ hours**

low-calorie cooking oil spray
2 oz **smoked Canadian bacon**, trimmed of fat and chopped
1 **red onion**, chopped
½ teaspoon **smoked hot paprika** or **chili powder**
1¼ cups **chicken stock**
16 oz can **reduced-sugar baked beans**
14½ oz **extra-lean sausages**
1 **red bell pepper**, cored, seeded, and chopped
2⅔ cups diced **pumpkin**
2 **celery sticks**, thickly sliced
2 **sage sprigs** or ½ teaspoon **dried sage**
salt and **pepper**

Preheat the slow cooker if necessary. Spray a large skillet with a little low-calorie cooking oil spray and place over high heat until hot. Add the bacon and onion and fry for 4–5 minutes, stirring until just beginning to brown. Stir in the paprika, then pour in the stock and baked beans. Season to taste, then bring to a boil, stirring.

Arrange the sausages in a single layer in the bottom of the slow cooker pot, top with the red pepper, pumpkin, celery, and sage, then pour over the hot stock and beans. Cover and cook on High for 5–6 hours. Stir the stew, spoon into shallow bowls, and serve.

For hearty winter chicken stew, follow the recipe above, using 1¼ lb boneless, skinless chicken thighs instead of the sausages, and browning them with the bacon and onion. Add to the slow cooker pot with the vegetables, pour over the hot stock and beans, cover, and cook on Low for 7–8 hours. **Calories per serving 315**

braised trout with warm puy lentils

Calories per serving **279**
Serves **4**
Preparation time **20 minutes**
Cooking time **2½–3 hours**

14½ oz can **Puy lentils**,
  drained
2 tablespoons **balsamic
  vinegar**
4 **scallions**, chopped
3 **tomatoes**, chopped
4 thick **trout steaks**, 5 oz each
finely grated zest and juice of
  ½ **lemon**
leaves from 2–3 **thyme sprigs**
large pinch of **dried red
  pepper flakes**
⅔ cup hot **fish stock**
salt and **pepper**
1¼ cups **arugula leaves**,
  to serve

Preheat the slow cooker if necessary. Place the lentils in the slow cooker pot, then stir in the balsamic vinegar, scallions, and tomatoes.

Arrange the trout steaks on top in a single layer, then sprinkle with the lemon zest and juice, thyme leaves, and pepper flakes and season to taste. Pour the stock around the trout steaks, then cover and cook on Low for 2½–3 hours or until the trout is cooked through and flakes easily when pressed with a small knife.

Divide the arugula leaves among 4 serving plates. Arrange the trout and lentils on top and spoon over a little of the stock. Serve immediately.

For smoked cod & spinach salad, follow the recipe above, using 1½ cups sliced button mushrooms instead of the tomatoes, and 4 thick smoked cod loin steaks, 5 oz each, instead of the trout. After cooking, stir 1 cup baby spinach leaves into the lentil mixture and serve each portion topped with a poached egg. **Calories per serving 228**

turkey with cranberries & pumpkin

Calories per serving **270**
**(not including steamed
   greens and broccoli)**
Serves **4**
Preparation time **20 minutes**
Cooking time **6¼–8¼ hours**

low-calorie cooking oil spray
1 lb **turkey breast**, diced
1 **onion**, chopped
2 teaspoons **all-purpose flour**
1¼ cups **chicken stock**
juice of 1 large **orange**
½ teaspoon **ground allspice**
¼ cup **dried cranberries**
1 lb peeled **pumpkin**, cut into
   1 inch cubes
salt and **pepper**

Preheat the slow cooker if necessary. Spray a large skillet with a little low-calorie cooking oil spray and place over high heat until hot. Add the turkey, a few pieces at a time until all the turkey is in the pan. Add the onion and cook for 5 minutes, stirring and turning the turkey pieces until golden.

Sprinkle in the flour and stir well. Add the stock, orange juice, spice, and cranberries and season with salt and pepper to taste. Bring to the boil, stirring.

Place the pumpkin in the slow cooker pot and pour the turkey mixture on top, pushing the turkey pieces into the liquid. Cover and cook on Low for 6–8 hours, until the turkey is cooked through. Spoon into shallow dishes and serve with steamed green beans and broccoli, if desired.

For turkey curry with golden raisins & pumpkin, follow the recipe above but omit the allspice and cranberries and add 1 tablespoon medium-hot curry powder and 2 tablespoons golden raisins instead.
Calories per serving 279

chunky chicken & basil stew

Calories per serving **262**
Serves **4**
Preparation time **20 minutes**
Cooking time **8½–10¾ hours**

low-calorie cooking oil spray
1¼ lb boneless, skinless
  chicken thighs, each cut
  into 3 pieces
1 **onion**, chopped
2 small **carrots**, finely diced
2 teaspoons **all-purpose flour**
1½ cups **chicken stock**
½ cup **basil leaves**, torn, plus
  extra to garnish
⅔ cup **frozen peas**, defrosted
7 oz **broccolini**, stems cut into
  3 or 4 pieces
1½ cups **green beans**,
  thickly sliced
salt and **pepper**

Preheat the slow cooker if necessary. Spray a large skillet with a little low-calorie cooking oil spray and place over high heat until hot. Add the chicken, a few pieces at a time until all the chicken is in the pan, and cook for 5 minutes, stirring, until golden. Transfer to the slow cooker pot using a slotted spoon.

Add a little more low-calorie cooking oil spray to the pan if necessary, then cook the onion for 4–5 minutes, until just beginning to soften. Stir in the carrots and flour, then add the stock and bring to a boil, stirring. Add the basil, season to taste, and pour over the chicken. Cover and cook on Low for 8–10 hours, until the chicken is tender and cooked through.

Add the peas, broccolini and green beans, cover again and cook on High for 15–30 minutes, until the vegetables are tender. Serve in shallow bowls, garnished with extra basil.

For chunky chicken with 30 garlic cloves, brown 1¼ lb boneless, skinless chicken thighs, each cut into 3 pieces, in a skillet and place in the slow cooker pot with 30 unpeeled garlic cloves. Follow the recipe above, using 8 oz small peeled shallots instead of the onion and carrot, and 3 thyme sprigs and 2 teaspoons Dijon mustard instead of the basil. Cook as above, omitting the green vegetables, and serve sprinkled with chopped parsley. **Calories per serving 225**

caribbean brown stew trout

Calories per serving **293**
Serves **4**
Preparation time **20 minutes**
Cooking time **1½—2 hours**

4 small **trout**, gutted, heads
   and fins removed and well
   rinsed with cold water
1 teaspoon **ground allspice**
1 teaspoon **paprika**
1 teaspoon **ground cilantro**
2 tablespoons **olive oil**
6 **scallions**, thickly sliced
1 **red bell pepper**, cored,
   seeded, and thinly sliced
2 **tomatoes**, coarsely chopped
½ **red hot bonnet** or other **red
   chile**, seeded and chopped
2 sprigs of **thyme**
1¼ cups **fish stock**
salt and **pepper**

Preheat the slow cooker if necessary. Slash the trout on each side 2–3 times with a sharp knife. Mix the spices and a little salt and pepper on a plate, then dip each side of the trout in the spice mix.

Heat the oil in a skillet, add the trout, and fry until browned on both sides but not cooked all the way through. Drain and arrange in the slow cooker pot so that they fit snugly in a single layer.

Add the remaining ingredients to the skillet with any spices left on the plate and bring to a boil, stirring. Pour over the trout, then cover with the lid and cook on High for 1½–2 hours or until the fish breaks into flakes when pressed in the center with a knife.

Lift the fish carefully out of the slow cooker pot using a spatula and transfer to shallow dishes. Spoon the sauce over and serve.

For brown stew chicken, use 8 chicken thigh joints instead of the trout. Slash and dip in the spice mix as above. Fry in the olive oil until browned, then drain and transfer to the slow cooker pot. Heat the vegetables as above using 1½ cups chicken stock instead of fish stock, season, then cook with the chicken joints in the slow cooker on Low for 8–10 hours. Thicken the sauce if desired with 4 teaspoons cornstarch mixed with a little water, stir into the sauce and cook for 15 minutes more. **Calories per serving 331**

coconut, pumpkin & chickpea curry

Calories per serving **236**
Serves **4**
Preparation time **25 minutes**
Cooking time **6¼–8¼ hours**

2 **onions**
2 **garlic cloves**, halved
1½ inch piece of **fresh ginger root**, sliced
1 **red chile**, quartered and seeded
low-calorie cooking oil spray
1½ tablespoons **medium curry powder**
1 teaspoon **fennel seeds**, coarsely crushed
¾ cup **full-fat coconut milk**
1¼ cups **vegetable stock**
2 teaspoons **granular sweetener**
1 lb 5 oz peeled **pumpkin**, cut into 1½ inch chunks
15 oz can **chickpeas**, drained
1 teaspoon **black mustard seeds**
½ cup **fresh cilantro**, coarsely torn
juice of 1 **lime**
salt and **pepper**

Preheat the slow cooker if necessary. Quarter 1 of the onions and place with the garlic, ginger, and chile in a food processor and blitz until very finely chopped. Alternatively, chop the ingredients finely with a knife. Spray a large skillet with a little low-calorie cooking oil spray and place over high heat until hot. Add the onion paste and cook for 2 minutes, then stir in the curry powder and fennel seeds.

Add the coconut milk, stock, and sweetener, then season to taste. Bring to a boil, stirring. Place the pumpkin and chickpeas in the slow cooker pot and pour the coconut mixture on top. Cover and cook on Low for 6–8 hours, until the pumpkin is tender.

Make a crispy onion topping by slicing the remaining onion. Heat a little low-calorie cooking oil spray in a clean skillet and cook the onion over medium heat for 5 minutes until softened. Stir in the mustard seeds and cook for a few minutes more until the onion is golden and crispy. Stir the cilantro and lime juice into the curry, spoon into bowls, and serve topped with the crispy onions.

For creamy coconut, eggplant & chickpea curry, follow the recipe above, using 1¼ lb eggplants, trimmed and diced, instead of the pumpkin. **Calories per serving 246**

tandoori chicken

Calories per serving **208**
Serves **4**
Preparation time **20 minutes,
plus marinating**
Cooking time **3¼–4¼ hours**

⅔ cup **0% fat Greek yogurt**
1½ inch piece of **fresh ginger
root**, grated
3 tablespoons chopped **fresh
cilantro leaves**
1 tablespoon **medium-hot
curry powder**
½ teaspoon **ground turmeric**
1 teaspoon **paprika**
1¼ lb boneless, skinless
chicken thighs, cut into
chunks
juice of ½ **lemon**
low-calorie cooking oil spray
salt and **pepper**

To serve
1½ cups **mixed salad greens**
¼ **cucumber**, diced
small handful of **fresh cilantro
leaves**
juice of ½ **lemon**

Place the yogurt in a mixing bowl and stir in the ginger, cilantro, curry powder, turmeric, and paprika. Toss the chicken with the lemon juice, season lightly with salt and pepper, and stir into the yogurt mixture until evenly coated. Cover the bowl and chill overnight.

Preheat the slow cooker if necessary. Stir the chicken mixture, then transfer to the slow cooker pot in an even layer. Cover and cook on High for 3–4 hours or until the chicken is tender and cooked through. (The yogurt will separate during cooking but this will not affect the taste.)

Spray a large skillet with a little low-calorie cooking oil spray and place over high heat until hot. Transfer the chicken to the skillet, a few pieces at a time until all the chicken is in the pan, and cook for 2–3 minutes, turning once, until golden on both sides. This step can be omitted if you are short of time.

Toss the salad greens, cucumber, and cilantro leaves with the lemon juice, arrange on serving plates and top with the chicken.

For garlicky tandoori chicken, add 3 finely chopped garlic cloves to the yogurt and spice mixture and continue as above. **Calories per serving 209**

chile, mushroom & tomato ragu

Calories per serving **295**
Serves **4**
Preparation time **20 minutes**
Cooking time **7¼–8¼ hours**

1 tablespoon **olive oil**
1 **red onion**, coarsely chopped
2 **garlic cloves**, finely chopped
1 teaspoon **paprika**
½ teaspoon **dried red pepper flakes**
1 teaspoon **dried Mediterranean herbs**
1½ cups **tomato puree** or **tomato sauce**
2 teaspoons **granular sweetener**
10 oz small **button mushrooms**
1¼ cups **cherry tomatoes**
salt and **pepper**

To serve
7 oz **dried penne pasta**
large pinch of **dried red pepper flakes** (optional)
handful of **arugula leaves**

Preheat the slow cooker if necessary. Heat the oil in a large skillet over medium heat until hot, add the onion, and cook for 4–5 minutes, stirring, until just beginning to soften. Add the garlic, paprika, and pepper flakes, then the dried herbs, tomato puree or sauce, and sweetener. Season to taste and bring to the boil.

Place the mushrooms and cherry tomatoes in the slow cooker pot, pour over the hot tomato sauce mixture and stir well. Cover and cook on Low for 7–8 hours.

Cook the pasta in a saucepan of lightly salted boiling water according to package instructions until tender. Drain and stir into the ragu, then spoon into shallow bowls and sprinkle with a few extra dried red pepper flakes, if desired, and top with the arugula. Serve immediately.

For zucchini & tomato arrabiata, follow the recipe above, using 1 cup diced zucchini and 1 cored, seeded, and diced red bell pepper instead of the mushrooms. **Calories per serving 307**

corn & smoked cod chowder

Calories per serving **207**
Serves **4**
Preparation time **20 minutes**
Cooking time **2¼–3¼ hours**

low-calorie cooking oil spray
1 **leek**, thinly sliced
2 oz **smoked Canadian bacon**, trimmed of fat and diced
1½ cups finely diced **potato**
1¼ cups finely diced **celeriac**
⅓ cup **frozen sweetcorn kernels**
2 cups **fish stock**
1 **bay leaf**
8 oz **smoked cod fillet**
¾ cup **skim milk**
3 tablespoons **reduced-fat cream cheese**
salt and **pepper**
chopped **parsley**, to garnish

Preheat the slow cooker if necessary. Spray a large skillet with a little low-calorie cooking oil spray and place over medium heat until hot. Add the white leek slices (reserving the green slices) and the bacon and cook for 3–4 minutes, until the leeks have softened and the bacon is just beginning to brown.

Add the potato, celeriac, corn, and stock. Bring to a boil, stirring, then add the bay leaf and season to taste. Transfer to the slow cooker pot, arrange the fish on top and press the fish into the liquid. Cover and cook on High for 2–3 hours, until the potatoes and celeriac are tender and the fish flakes easily when pressed with a small knife. Transfer the fish to a plate, remove the skin and bones and break into pieces.

Stir the milk and cream cheese into the slow cooker pot, then stir in the reserved green leek slices and the flaked fish. Cover again and cook for 15 minutes, until the leeks are tender. Ladle into bowls and serve garnished with the chopped parsley.

For salmon & crab chowder, follow the recipe above, using 8 oz salmon fillet instead of the smoked cod. Cook as above, stirring in a 1½ oz can of dark crab meat for the last 15 minutes of cooking time. **Calories per serving 249**

baba ganoush

Calories per serving **239**
Serves **4**
Preparation time **20 minutes**
Cooking time **3–4 hours**

1 large **eggplant**, 10 oz,
   halved lengthwise
1 tablespoon **olive oil**
2 tablespoons **0% fat Greek
   yogurt**
3 tablespoons chopped **fresh
   cilantro leaves**
1 large **garlic clove**, finely
   chopped
juice of ½ **lemon**
seeds from ¼ **pomegranate**
salt and **pepper**

To serve
4 **pita breads**
1 **red bell pepper**, cored,
   seeded, and cut into batons
½ **cucumber**, seeded and cut
   into batons

Preheat the slow cooker if necessary. Cut criss-cross lines over the cut side of each eggplant half, rub with salt and pepper, then drizzle with the oil. Arrange, cut sides down, in the base of the slow cooker pot, cover and cook on High for 3–4 hours or until the eggplants are soft. Let cool.

Use a spoon to scoop the flesh out of the eggplant skins and chop it coarsely. Place in a mixing bowl with the yogurt, cilantro leaves, garlic, and lemon juice. Season to taste, spoon into a serving dish, and sprinkle with the pomegranate seeds.

Warm the pita breads under a preheated hot broiler, then cut into thick strips. Arrange on a serving plate with the pepper and cucumber batons and serve with the baba ganoush.

For broiled steaks with eggplant sauce, make the baba ganoush following the recipe above. Trim the fat from 4 sirloin steaks, 4 oz each, and season to taste. Spray with a little low-calorie cooking oil spray and cook on a preheated hot ridged grill pan for 2–3 minutes, turning once, or until cooked to your desire. Serve the steaks with the baba ganoush and an arugula salad tossed with lemon juice. **Calories per serving 294**

tapenade-topped cod

Calories per serving **246**
Serves **4**
Preparation time **15 minutes**
Cooking time **3½–4 hours**

¾ cup **tomato puree** or
  tomato sauce
4 cups **spinach**, rinsed and
  drained
6 oz **tomatoes**, coarsely
  chopped
2 oz **chorizo**, diced
4 skinless **cod steaks**,
  5 oz each
½ cup **green olives stuffed
  with hot pimento**
small handful of **basil leaves**,
  plus extra to garnish
salt and **pepper**

Preheat the slow cooker if necessary. Spoon the tomato puree or sauce over the bottom of the slow cooker pot, then arrange the spinach, tomatoes, and chorizo in an even layer on top. Season to taste and place the fish steaks on top in a single layer, then season again.

Place the olives and basil in a food processor and blitz until finely chopped, or chop with a knife. Spread the mixture over the cod steaks, then cover and cook on Low for 3½ –4 hours, until the fish is bright white and flakes easily when pressed with a small knife. Serve garnished with extra basil.

For herb-topped cod, mix ½ cup finely chopped parsley and ⅓ cup finely chopped basil with ½ teaspoon crushed cumin seeds and the grated zest of 1 lemon. Follow the recipe above, using this herb mixture to spread over the cod steaks before cooking instead of the olives and basil. **Calories per serving 249**

hot quinoa & pepper salad

Calories per serving **202**
Serves **4**
Preparation time **15 minutes**
Cooking time **3–4 hours**

3 **bell peppers**, cored,
  seeded, and cut into chunks
2 **celery sticks**, sliced
2 **zucchini**, halved lengthwise
  and thickly sliced
8 oz **plum tomatoes**, coarsely
  chopped
2 **garlic cloves**, finely chopped
½ cup **quinoa and bulgur
  wheat grain mix**
¼ cup **red wine**
1¼ cups hot **vegetable stock**
1 tablespoon **tomato paste**
1 teaspoon **granular
  sweetener**
½ cup **basil leaves**, coarsely
  torn
salt and **pepper**

Preheat the slow cooker if necessary. Place the peppers, celery, zucchini, and tomatoes in the slow cooker pot and sprinkle over the garlic and grain mix.

Mix the red wine with the stock, tomato paste, and sweetener, season with salt and pepper to taste, and pour into the slow cooker pot. Stir the ingredients together, then cover and cook on High for 3–4 hours, until the vegetables have softened and the grains have absorbed the liquid.

Stir the salad, then divide among 4 shallow bowls and serve topped with the torn basil leaves.

For hot quinoa & shrimp salad, follow the recipe above to make the quinoa salad and divide among 4 bowls. Omit the basil and divide 2½ cups mixed spinach, watercress, and arugula leaves and 6 oz cooked peeled shrimp between the bowls. **Calories per serving 257**

asian turkey with rainbow chard

Calories per serving **234 (not including rice or noodles)**
Serves **4**
Preparation time **20 minutes**
Cooking time **8½–9¾ hours**

low-calorie cooking oil spray
1 lb **turkey breast**, diced
1 **onion**, chopped
2 **garlic cloves**, finely chopped
7 oz **closed-cap mushrooms**, sliced
2 cups **chicken stock**
1 inch piece of **fresh ginger root**, chopped
2 tablespoons **soy sauce**
1 tablespoon **tamarind paste**
1 tablespoon **tomato paste**
1 tablespoon **cornstarch**
7 oz **rainbow chard**, thickly sliced

Preheat the slow cooker if necessary. Spray a large skillet with a little low-calorie cooking oil spray and place over high heat until hot. Add the turkey, a few pieces at a time until all the turkey is in the pan, and cook for 5 minutes, stirring, until golden. Transfer to the slow cooker pot using a slotted spoon.

Add a little extra low-calorie cooking oil spray to the skillet, if necessary, and cook the onion for 4–5 minutes, until softened. Stir in the garlic and mushrooms and cook for 2–3 minutes more. Add the stock, ginger, soy sauce, tamarind, and tomato paste, season to taste and bring to a boil, stirring. Pour over the turkey, cover, and cook on Low for 8–9 hours, until the turkey is cooked through.

Mix the cornstarch to a smooth paste with a little cold water and stir into the turkey mixture. Arrange the chard on top, cover again, and cook on High for 15–30 minutes, until tender. Spoon into bowls and serve with rice or noodles, if desired.

For black bean turkey, follow the recipe above to brown the turkey and fry the onion. Add the mushrooms to the skillet with a 16 oz jar of black bean cooking sauce and bring to a boil. Transfer to the slow cooker pot and cook as above. Stir-fry 9 oz prepared stir-fry vegetables in a little low-calorie cooking oil spray to serve with the turkey. **Calories per serving 294**

smoky sweet potato & quorn chili

Calories per serving **299**
Serves **4**
Preparation time **20 minutes**
Cooking time **7¼–8¼ hours**

1–2 small **dried smoked
    chipotle chiles**
¼ cup boiling **water**
low-calorie cooking oil spray
1 **onion**, chopped
2 **garlic cloves**, finely chopped
1 teaspoon **ground cumin**
1 teaspoon **paprika**
2 x 14½ oz cans **diced
    tomatoes**
15 oz can **red kidney beans**,
    rinsed and drained
1 tablespoon **Worcestershire
    sauce** (optional)
11½ oz **Quorn grounds**
10 oz **sweet potato**, cut into
    1 inch cubes
salt and **pepper**

Salsa

½ **red onion**, finely chopped
3 tablespoons chopped **fresh
    cilantro**
2 **tomatoes**, halved, seeded,
    and diced

Preheat the slow cooker if necessary. Place the dried chiles in a small bowl, pour over the boiling water and let stand for 10 minutes.

Spray a large skillet with a little low-calorie cooking oil spray and place over medium heat until hot. Add the onion, cook for 4–5 minutes, until softened, then add the garlic, cumin, and paprika. Stir in the tomatoes, kidney beans, and Worcestershire sauce, if using, then the Quorn and sweet potato. Season with salt and pepper to taste.

Finely chop the chiles, then stir into the Quorn mixture with the soaking water. Bring to a boil, stirring, then transfer to the slow cooker pot. Cover and cook on Low for 7–8 hours until the sweet potato is tender. Mix the salsa ingredients together, then sprinkle over the chili to serve.

For sweet potato & soy curry, follow the recipe above, omitting the chipotle chiles. Add 1 teaspoon ground turmeric, 1 teaspoon garam masala, and ½ teaspoon dried red pepper flakes with the cumin and paprika, and a 14½ oz can lentils, drained, when adding 11½ oz textured vegetable protein. Cook as above, then add ⅔ cup frozen peas and ¼ cup chopped fresh cilantro, cover again, and cook on High for 15 minutes. **Calories per serving 299**

eggplant parmigiana

Calories per serving **221**
Serves **4**
Preparation time **15 minutes**
Cooking time **4¼–5¼ hours**

1 tablespoon **olive oil**
1 **onion**, chopped
2 **garlic cloves**, finely chopped
2 cups diced **tomatoes**
14½ oz can **diced tomatoes**
small handful of **basil**, torn,
    plus extra to garnish
2 teaspoons **granular**
    sweetener
2 teaspoons **cornstarch**
2 large **eggplants**, sliced
¾ cup shredded **sharp**
    cheddar cheese
salt and **pepper**
2 tablespoons finely grated
    Parmesan cheese,
    to garnish

Preheat the slow cooker if necessary. Heat the oil in a large skillet over medium heat, add the onion, and cook for 4–5 minutes, until just beginning to soften. Add the garlic, fresh tomatoes, canned tomatoes, basil, and sweetener. Mix the cornstarch to a smooth paste with a little cold water and stir into the sauce. Season with salt and pepper to taste and bring to a boil, stirring.

Spoon a little of the tomato sauce over the bottom of the slow cooker pot and arrange one-third of the eggplant slices, overlapping, on top. Spoon over a thin layer of the sauce and sprinkle with a little shredded cheddar. Repeat to make 3 eggplant layers, finishing with a generous layer of sauce and shredded cheddar.

Cover and cook on High for 4–5 hours until the eggplants are soft. Sprinkle with the Parmesan and extra basil and serve.

For mushroom parmigiana, follow the recipe above to make the tomato sauce, then layer in the slow cooker pot with 8 large flat mushrooms, in 2 layers, and the cheddar. Cook and serve as above. **Calories per serving 235**

easy cauliflower dahl

Calories per serving **211**
Serves **4**
Preparation time **15 minutes**
Cooking time **3–4 hours**

1 cup **dried red lentils**, rinsed
in cold water and drained
3 cups hot **water**
2 teaspoons **medium curry
powder**
½ teaspoon **salt**
pepper

Spiced cauliflower
13 oz **cauliflower**, cut into
small florets
6 tablespoons **water**
1 **onion**, thinly sliced
low-calorie cooking oil spray
1 teaspoon **cumin seeds**,
coarsely crushed
1 teaspoon **ground turmeric**
1 teaspoon **garam masala**

Preheat the slow cooker if necessary. Place the lentils, hot water, curry powder, and salt in the slow cooker pot, then season with pepper. Cover and cook on High for 3–4 hours or until the lentils are soft.

Meanwhile, place the cauliflower in a large skillet with the water, cover, and cook over medium heat for 5 minutes, until the cauliflower is almost tender. Drain off any excess water, then add the onion and a little low-calorie cooking oil spray, increase the heat and cook for 2–3 minutes, stirring.

Sprinkle the cumin, turmeric, and garam masala over the cauliflower and cook, stirring, for 4–5 minutes, until the cauliflower is golden brown. Season to taste. Stir the lentil dahl, spoon into shallow bowls and top with the spiced cauliflower.

For easy eggplant & mushroom dahl, follow the recipe above to cook the lentil dahl. Spray a large skillet with a little low-calorie cooking oil spray, add 1 large diced eggplant and 1½ cups sliced button mushrooms and cook over medium heat for 2–3 minutes, until beginning to soften. Add a little more low-calorie cooking oil spray, then the cumin, turmeric, and garam masala as above and continue to cook until the eggplant is soft. Spoon over the dahl and sprinkle with chopped cilantro. **Calories per serving 201**

lentil tagine with pomegranate

Calories per serving **276**
Serves **4**
Preparation time **15 minutes**
Cooking time **4–5 hours**

1 tablespoon **olive oil**
1 **onion**, chopped
2 inch piece of **fresh ginger root**, finely chopped
3 **garlic cloves**, finely chopped
2 teaspoons **cumin seeds**, crushed
1 teaspoon **cilantro seeds**, crushed
1 cup **dried Puy lentils**
2 **celery sticks**, sliced
1 cup **cherry tomatoes**, halved
2 cups hot **vegetable stock**
juice of **1 lemon**
¼ cup **flat-leaf parsley**, coarsely chopped
3 tablespoons **mint**, coarsely chopped
salt and **pepper**

To serve
½ cup **0% fat Greek yogurt**
1 tablespoon **harissa**
seeds from ½ **pomegranate**

Preheat the slow cooker if necessary. Heat the oil in a large skillet over medium heat, add the onion, and cook for 4–5 minutes, until just beginning to soften. Stir in the ginger, garlic, cumin, and cilantro seeds.

Place the lentils in a sieve and rinse under cold running water. Drain and transfer to the slow cooker pot. Spoon the onion mixture on top, then add the celery and tomatoes. Pour over the hot stock, season with salt and pepper to taste, cover, and cook on High for 4–5 hours, until the lentils are tender.

Stir in the lemon juice and herbs and spoon into bowls. Top with the yogurt and harissa, then sprinkle with the pomegranate seeds and serve immediately.

For chickpea & lentil tagine, follow the recipe above, adding ½ teaspoon chili powder with the other spices and using ½ cup Puy lentils and a 15 oz can of chickpeas, drained, instead of 1 cup lentils. Omit the mint and pomegranate, but stir in 1 cup chopped parsley and serve topped with the yogurt and harissa. **Calories per serving 256**

hoppin' john rice

Calories per serving **292**
Serves **4**
Preparation time **15 minutes,
  plus soaking**
Cooking time **1½–2 hours**

1 cup **white basmati rice**,
  soaked in cold water for
  10 minutes
4 **scallions**, chopped
1 **red bell pepper**, cored,
  seeded, and diced
5 oz peeled **pumpkin** or
  butternut squash, cut into
  ½ inch dice
2 **tomatoes**, diced
15 oz can **black-eyed peas**,
  drained
leaves from 2 **thyme sprigs**
½–1 **red chile**, seeded
½ teaspoon **ground allspice**
½ teaspoon **salt**
3 cups boiling **water**
½ cup **fresh cilantro**, finely
  chopped
pepper

Preheat the slow cooker if necessary. Place the soaked rice in a sieve and rinse under cold running water. Drain and place in the slow cooker pot with the scallions, red pepper, pumpkin or butternut squash, tomatoes, peas, thyme, and chile, to taste.

Stir the allspice and salt into the boiling water and pour over the rice. Season generously with black pepper. Cover and cook on High for 1½–2 hours until the rice is tender and has absorbed the water, stirring once during cooking and adding a little more hot water if the rice is too dry. Add the cilantro and fluff up the rice with a fork before serving.

For pumpkin rice, place the soaked and rinsed rice in the slow cooker pot with the scallions, 2½ cups peeled and diced pumpkin, 2 chopped garlic cloves, leaves from 2 thyme sprigs, 1 inch piece of fresh ginger root, grated, and ½–1 red chile. Pour over 3 cups hot water, season generously and cook as above. Stir in the chopped cilantro just before serving.
Calories per serving 248

moroccan meatballs

Calories per serving **245 (not including the couscous)**
Serves **4**
Preparation time **30 minutes**
Cooking time **6¼–8¼ hours**

1 lb **ground turkey breast**
½ cup drained canned **green lentils**
1 **egg yolk**
1 tablespoon **olive oil**
1 **onion**, sliced
2 **garlic cloves**, finely chopped
1 teaspoon **ground turmeric**
1 teaspoon **ground cilantro**
½ teaspoon **ground cumin**
½ teaspoon **ground cinnamon**
1 inch piece of **fresh ginger root**, finely chopped
14½ oz can **diced tomatoes**
⅔ cup **chicken stock**
salt and **pepper**

Preheat the slow cooker if necessary. Place the turkey in a bowl with the lentils and egg yolk, season with salt and pepper to taste and mix well. Shape the mixture into 20 small balls using wetted hands.

Heat the oil in a large skillet over high heat, add the meatballs, and cook, stirring, until browned but not cooked through. Transfer to the slow cooker pot using a slotted spoon. Add the onion to the pan and cook over medium heat for 5 minutes until softened, then stir in the garlic, spices, and ginger and cook for 1 minute.

Stir in the tomatoes and stock, season to taste, and bring to a boil, stirring. Pour over the meatballs, cover, and cook on Low for 6–8 hours or until the meatballs are cooked through. Stir, then spoon into shallow bowls and serve with lemon couscous, if desired.

For lemon couscous, to serve as an accompaniment, place 1 cup couscous in a large bowl with 2 cups boiling water, the grated zest and juice of 1 lemon, and 2 tablespoons olive oil. Season to taste, cover, and let stand for 5 minutes. Fluff up with a fork and stir in a small bunch of chopped cilantro. **Calories per serving 240**

carrot & cumin soup

Calories per serving **235**
Serves **4**
Preparation time **20 minutes**
Cooking time **7–8 hours**

1 tablespoon **sunflower oil**
1 large **onion**, chopped
1 ¼ lb **carrots**, thinly sliced
1 ½ teaspoons **cumin seeds**,
  coarsely crushed
1 teaspoon **ground turmeric**
¼ cup **long-grain rice**
5 cups **vegetable stock**
salt and **pepper**

To serve
⅔ cup **plain yogurt**
4 teaspoons **mango chutney**
4 ready-to-serve **pappadams**

Preheat the slow cooker if necessary. Heat the oil in a large skillet over medium heat, add the onion and cook, stirring, for 5 minutes, until softened. Stir in the carrots, cumin seeds, and turmeric and cook for 2–3 minutes until the onions start to color.

Stir in the rice, then add the stock, season with salt and pepper to taste, and bring to a boil. Pour into the slow cooker pot, cover, and cook on Low for 7–8 hours or until the carrots are tender.

Puree the soup in a blender or with a hand-held immersion blender until smooth, then adjust the seasoning if necessary and ladle the soup into bowls. Top with spoonfuls of yogurt and a little mango chutney and serve with the pappadams.

For spiced parsnip soup, follow the recipe above, replacing the carrots with 1 ¼ lb halved and thinly sliced parsnips. Use 1 teaspoon ground cumin, 1 teaspoon ground coriander, and a 1 ½ inch piece of fresh ginger root, finely chopped, instead of the cumin seeds. Continue as above and serve with the yogurt, mango chutney, and pappadams. **Calories per serving 275**

cajun red bean soup

Calories per serving **205**
Serves **6**
Preparation time **25 minutes,
  plus soaking**
Cooking time **8½–10½ hours**

¾ cup **dried red kidney
  beans**, soaked overnight in
  cold water
2 tablespoons **sunflower oil**
1 large **onion**, chopped
1 **red bell pepper**, cored,
  seeded, and diced
1 **carrot**, diced
1 **baking potato** 7 oz, diced
2–3 **garlic cloves**, chopped
  (optional)
2 teaspoons **Cajun spice
  mix** or ½–1 teaspoon **chili
  powder**
14½ oz can **diced tomatoes**
1 tablespoon packed **brown
  sugar**
4 cups hot **vegetable stock**
½ cup sliced **okra**
½ cup **green beans**, cut
  into short lengths
salt and **pepper**

Preheat the slow cooker if necessary. Drain and rinse the soaked beans, place in a saucepan, cover with fresh water and bring to a boil. Boil vigorously for 10 minutes, then drain in a sieve.

Meanwhile, heat the oil in a large skillet over medium heat, add the onion, and cook for 5 minutes, until softened. Add the red bell pepper, carrot, potato, and garlic (if using) and cook for 2–3 minutes. Stir in the Cajun spice, tomatoes, and sugar, season generously with salt and pepper and bring to a boil.

Transfer the mixture to the slow cooker pot, add the drained beans and hot stock and mix together. Cover and cook on Low for 8–10 hours, until the vegetables are tender.

Add the green vegetables, cover again, and cook for 30 minutes. Ladle the soup into bowls and serve.

For Hungarian paprika & red bean soup, follow the recipe above, using 1 teaspoon smoked paprika instead of the Cajun spice and omitting the green vegetables. Puree the soup and add a little boiling water if it is too thick. Ladle into soup bowls, top each portion with 2 tablespoons sour cream and a few caraway seeds, and serve immediately. **Calories per serving 252**

lamb & barley broth

Calories per serving **239**
Serves **4**
Preparation time **15 minutes**
Cooking time **8–10 hours**

2 tablespoons **butter**
1 tablespoon **sunflower oil**
1 **lamb sirloin chop** or 4 oz
   lamb tenderloin, diced
1 **onion**, chopped
1 small **leek**, chopped
3 cups mixed **parsnip**, **swede**,
   rutabaga, and **carrot**, cut
   into small dice
¼ cup **pearl barley**
5 cups **lamb** or **chicken stock**
¼ teaspoon **ground allspice**
2–3 **rosemary sprigs**
salt and **pepper**
chopped **parsley** or **chives**,
   to garnish

Preheat the slow cooker if necessary. Heat the butter and oil in a large skillet over high heat, add the lamb, onion, and leek and cook, stirring, for 5 minutes, until the lamb is lightly browned.

Stir in the root vegetables and barley, then add the stock, allspice, and rosemary. Season to taste and bring to a boil, stirring. Pour into the slow cooker pot, cover, and cook on Low for 8–10 hours or until the barley is tender.

Stir well, taste and adjust the seasoning, if necessary, then ladle the soup into bowls. Garnish with chopped herbs and serve.

For Hungarian chorba, follow the recipe above, adding 1 teaspoon smoked paprika, ¼ cup long-grain rice, and a few sprigs of dill instead of the pearl barley. Stir in 5 cups lamb stock, 2 tablespoons red wine vinegar, and 1 tablespoon light brown sugar. Season to taste, bring to a boil, and continue as above. Garnish with chopped dill and serve with rye bread, if desired. **Calories per serving 258**

minestrone soup

Calories per serving **267**
Serves **4**
Preparation time **15 minutes**
Cooking time **6½–8¾ hours**

1 tablespoon **olive oil**

1 **onion**, chopped

1 **carrot**, diced

2 **smoked bacon slices**,
  chopped

2 **garlic cloves**, finely chopped

4 **tomatoes**, skinned and
  chopped

2 **celery sticks**, diced

2 small **zucchini**, diced

1 tablespoon **prepared pesto**,
  plus 2 extra teaspoons
  to serve

5 cups **chicken** or **vegetable**
  stock

3 oz **purple sprouting**
  broccoli, cut into small
  pieces

3 tablespoons tiny **soup pasta**

salt and **pepper**

¼ cup freshly grated
  Parmesan cheese, to serve

Preheat the slow cooker if necessary. Heat the oil in a large skillet over high heat, add the onion, carrot, and bacon and cook for 5 minutes, until lightly browned. Add the garlic, then stir in the tomatoes, celery, and zucchini and cook for 1–2 minutes. Stir in the pesto and stock, season to taste, and bring to a boil, stirring.

Pour into the slow cooker pot, cover, and cook on Low for 6–8 hours or until the vegetables are tender. Add the broccoli and pasta, cover again, and cook on High for 15–30 minutes or until the pasta is tender.

Stir well, taste and adjust the seasoning, if necessary, then ladle the soup into bowls. Drizzle each bowl with ½ teaspoon of pesto, to taste. Sprinkle with the grated Parmesan and serve.

For curried vegetable & chicken soup, follow the recipe above, using 2 diced boneless, skinless chicken thighs instead of the bacon and 1 tablespoon mild curry paste instead of the pesto. Add 3 tablespoons basmati rice with 5 cups chicken stock and continue as above, omitting the pasta. Garnish with chopped fresh cilantro and serve with warm naan bread, if desired. **Calories per serving 255**

chunky beef & barley bro

Calories per serving **233**
Serves **4**
Preparation time **15 minutes**
Cooking time **5¼–6¼ hours**

10 oz **lean stewing beef**,
  diced
1⅔ cups finely diced
  rutabaga
1⅔ cups finely diced **carrot**
1 **onion**, finely chopped
¼ cup **pearl barley**
¼ cup **dried red lentils**
3¾ cups hot **beef stock**
1 teaspoon **dried mixed
  herbs**
1 teaspoon **dry mustard**
1 tablespoon **Worcestershire
  sauce**
1 cup thinly shredded **green
  cabbage**
salt and **pepper**

Preheat the slow cooker if necessary. Place the beef, rutabaga, carrot, and onion in the slow cooker pot, then add the pearl barley and lentils.

Mix the hot stock with the herbs, dry mustard, and Worcestershire sauce, then pour over the meat and vegetables. Stir well, season to taste, cover and cook on High for 5–6 hours, until the beef and barley are tender.

Stir, then add the cabbage. Cover again and cook for 15 minutes, until the cabbage is just tender. Ladle into bowls and serve.

For chicken & barley bro, follow the recipe above, using 10 oz boneless, skinless diced chicken thighs and 1 sliced leek instead of the beef and onion. Use 3¾ cups chicken stock instead of the beef stock, and ¼ cup pitted prunes, diced, instead of the Worcestershire sauce. Cook as above, adding the cabbage for the last 15 minutes. **Calories per serving 243**

coconut & rose rice pudding

Calories per serving **231**
Serves **4**
Preparation time **10 minutes**
Cooking time **2½–3 hours**

⅓ cup **short-grain rice**,
  rinsed in cold water and
  drained
¼ cup **sugar**
¼ cup **shredded coconut**
2½ cups **low-fat milk**
½–1 teaspoon **rose water**,
  to taste

To serve
1 cup **raspberries**
2 teaspoons **shredded
  coconut**

Preheat the slow cooker if necessary. Place the rice, sugar, and coconut in the slow cooker pot, add the milk and stir well. Cover and cook on High for 2½–3 hours, until the rice is tender.

Stir well, then add the rose water, to taste. Spoon into bowls, top with the raspberries and a little extra coconut, and serve immediately.

For vanilla & orange rice pudding, split 1 vanilla bean lengthwise and scrape out the seeds with a small knife. Follow the recipe above, adding the vanilla seeds to the rice and milk in the slow cooker pot with the vanilla pod and the finely grated zest of ½ orange. Stir well, cover, and cook as above. Stir again and remove the vanilla pod before serving with raspberries and a sprinkling of coconut. **Calories per serving 233**

sherried bread & butter puddings

Calories per serving **204**
Serves **4**
Preparation time **20 minutes**
Cooking time **3½–4 hours**

⅓ cup **mixed dried fruit**
2 tablespoons **sweet** or **dry sherry**
1 tablespoon **sunflower margarine**
3½ oz **white bread slices**
6 teaspoons **sugar**
¾ cup **skim milk**
1 teaspoon **vanilla extract**
2 **eggs**

Preheat the slow cooker if necessary. Place the dried fruit and sherry in a small saucepan and bring just to a boil. Remove from the heat and set aside.

Grease 4 x ¾ cup heatproof dishes with a little margarine, then use the rest to spread on the bread. Cut the bread into cubes, then layer in the dishes with the sherried fruit and 4 teaspoons of the sugar.

Beat the milk, vanilla, and eggs in a pitcher, then strain into the dishes. Cover with squares of greased foil and stand in the slow cooker pot. Pour hot water into the pot to come halfway up the sides of the dishes, then cover and cook on Low for 3½–4 hours or until the custard has set.

Sprinkle the tops of the puddings with the remaining sugar and brown with a cook's blow torch, or under a preheated hot broiler. Serve warm.

For Paddington puddings, spread 3½ oz white bread slices with 1 tablespoon sunflower margarine and 2 tablespoons reduced-sugar fine-shred marmalade. Layer in the dishes with ⅓ cup dried fruit. Mix the milk, vanilla, and eggs, as above, with 2 teaspoons sugar and pour over the bread mixture. Cook and finish as above. **Calories per serving 214**

chocolate crème caramels

Calories per serving **251**
Serves **4**
Preparation time **25 minutes,
plus cooling and chilling**
Cooking time **3–4 hours**

2 tablespoons unsweetened
cocoa powder
2 teaspoons **instant coffee
powder**
2 tablespoons boiling **water**
2 **eggs**
2 **egg yolks**
2 tablespoons **granular
sweetener**
2 cups **low-fat milk**

Caramel
½ cup **granulated sugar**
6 tablespoons cold **water**
2 tablespoons boiling **water**

Preheat the slow cooker if necessary. For the caramel, place the granulated sugar in a heavy saucepan with the cold water. Cook over low heat, without stirring, until the sugar has completely dissolved. Increase the heat and boil for 5–8 minutes or until the syrup turns a rich golden brown, but before it becomes too dark.

Remove the pan from the heat and add the boiling water, taking care as the syrup can spit. Tilt the pan to mix, then pour into 4 x ¾ cup metal pudding basins. Holding the basins with a cloth, tilt them to swirl the caramel over the bottom and sides. Cool for 10 minutes.

Place the cocoa, coffee, and boiling water in a mixing bowl and stir to a smooth paste. Add the eggs, egg yolks, and sweetener and stir until smooth.

Pour the milk into the empty caramel pan and bring just to a boil. Gradually whisk it into the cocoa mixture, then strain through a sieve into a pitcher. Pour into the basins, cover the tops with greased foil, and put in the slow cooker pot.

Pour boiling water into the slow cooker pot to come halfway up the sides of the basins, cover, and cook on Low for 3–4 hours, until set. Remove from the slow cooker and let cool, then chill in the refrigerator for 3–4 hours or overnight. To serve, dip the molds in hot water, count to 10, loosen the edges with a round-bladed knife, then turn out onto shallow dishes.

For vanilla crème caramels, follow the recipe above to make the caramel and put it in the basins. Mix 2 eggs with 3 egg yolks, 2 tablespoons granular sweetener, and 1 teaspoon vanilla extract. Add the hot milk and continue as above. **Calories per serving 239**

brandied chocolate fondue

Calories per serving **220**
Serves **4**
Preparation time **10 minutes**
Cooking time **¾–1 hour**

3½ oz **dark chocolate**, broken
   into pieces
6 tablespoons **skim milk**
1 teaspoon **granular
   sweetener**
1 tablespoon **brandy**

To serve
3 cups **strawberries**, halved
   if large
1¼ cups **raspberries**
1 large **peach**, halved, pitted,
   and cut into chunks

Preheat the slow cooker if necessary. Place the chocolate, milk, and sweetener in a heatproof bowl, cover with a saucer and stand in the slow cooker pot. Pour boiling water into the slow cooker pot to come halfway up the sides of the bowl, cover, and cook on High for ¾–1 hour.

Remove the bowl from the slow cooker and stand on a large plate. Stir the fondue until smooth and glossy, then stir in the brandy.

Arrange the strawberries, raspberries, and peaches on the plate. Serve with fondue forks or wooden skewers for spearing the fruit and dipping into the fondue.

For white chocolate fondue, place 3½ oz white chocolate, broken into pieces, in a heatproof bowl with a few drops of vanilla extract and 6 tablespoons skim milk. Cook as above, then stir in 1 tablespoon Kirsch and serve with mixed berries. **Calories per serving 213**

pancakes with fruit compote

Calories per serving **258**
Serves **4**
Preparation time **15 minutes**
Cooking time **2–2½ hours**

10 oz ripe **red plums**, halved,
  pitted, and diced
1 **dessert apple**, quartered,
  cored, and diced
1 cup **blackberries**
¼ teaspoon **ground
  cinnamon**, plus extra to
  decorate
1 tablespoon **granular
  sweetener**
3 tablespoons **water**

Pancakes
⅔ cup **all-purpose flour**
1 **egg** and 1 **egg yolk**
¾ cup **skim milk**
1 teaspoon **sunflower** or
  vegetable oil

To serve
⅔ cup **fromage frais** or **low-
  fat plain yogurt**

Preheat the slow cooker if necessary. Place all the compote ingredients in the slow cooker pot, stir well, cover, and cook on High for 2–2½ hours, until the fruits have softened.

Make the pancake batter. Place the flour in a large bowl, create a well in the middle and add the egg, egg yolk, and milk. Whisk, starting from the center and gradually drawing the flour into the eggs and milk. Once all the flour is incorporated, beat until you have a smooth, thick batter. Let stand for 30 minutes.

Heat a 7-inch skillet over moderate heat, wipe it with oiled paper towel and ladle some of the pancake batter into the pan, tilting the pan to move the batter around for a thin and even layer. Let cook for at least 30 seconds before flipping the pancake over to cook on the other side. Transfer cooked pancakes to a plate. The batter will make four 7-inch pancakes. Alternatively, use 4 store-bought pancakes, 2 oz each.

Warm the pancakes and divide among 4 serving plates. Top with the fruit compote, then fold the pancakes in half and spoon the fromage frais on top. Sprinkle with a little extra cinnamon and serve immediately.

For orchard fruit sundaes, follow the recipe above to make the fruit compote and let cool. Spoon into 4 glasses, top with 1 cup fromage frais and drizzle each portion with 2 teaspoons maple syrup. **Calories per serving 163**

recipes
under 400
calories

all-in-one chicken casserole

Calories per serving **398**
Serves **4**
Preparation time **20 minutes**
Cooking time **8¼–10¼ hours**

low-calorie cooking oil spray
4 skinless **chicken legs**,
  1¾ lb in total
2 oz **smoked Canadian
  bacon**, trimmed of fat and
  chopped
10 oz **baby new potatoes**,
  thickly sliced
2 small **leeks**, thickly sliced
2 **celery sticks**, thickly sliced
2 **carrots**, sliced
2 teaspoons **all-purpose flour**
1 teaspoon **dried mixed
  herbs**
1 teaspoon **dry mustard**
2 cups **chicken stock**
½ cup sliced **curly kale**
salt and **pepper**

Spray a large skillet with a little low-calorie cooking oil spray and place over high heat until hot. Add the chicken and cook for 5 minutes, turning, until browned all over. Transfer to the slow cooker pot.

Add the bacon and potatoes to the skillet with a little extra low-calorie cooking oil spray and cook for 4–5 minutes, stirring, until the bacon is beginning to brown. Stir in the white leek slices (reserving the green slices), the celery, and carrots. Add the flour, herbs, and dry mustard and stir well.

Pour in the stock, season to taste, and bring to a boil, stirring. Spoon over the chicken, cover, and cook on Low for 8–10 hours or until the chicken is thoroughly cooked and the meat juices run clear when the thickest parts of the leg are pierced with a sharp knife.

Add the reserved green leek slices and the kale to the slow cooker pot, cover, and cook for 15 minutes until the vegetables are just tender. Serve in shallow bowls.

For chicken hotpot, follow the main recipe to make the chicken mixture, omitting the new potatoes and carrots. Transfer to the slow cooker pot and cover with 10 oz scrubbed and thinly sliced baking potatoes and 2 thinly sliced carrots, arranging the slices alternately overlapping. Spray with low-calorie cooking oil spray, season to taste, then cook as above. After cooking, brown the top under the broiler, if desired. **Calories per serving 403**

beet & caraway risotto

Calories per serving **325**
Serves **4**
Preparation time **15 minutes**
Cooking time **5–6 hours**

1 cup **long-grain brown rice**
2 cups diced **beets**
1 **red onion**, finely chopped
2 **garlic cloves**, finely chopped
1 teaspoon **caraway seeds**
2 teaspoons **tomato paste**
5 cups hot **vegetable stock**
salt and **pepper**

To serve
¼ cup **Greek yogurt**
4 oz **smoked salmon slices**
handful of **arugula leaves**

Preheat the slow cooker if necessary. Place the rice in a sieve, rinse well under cold running water and drain well.

Place the beets, onion, and garlic in the slow cooker pot, add the drained rice, caraway seeds, and tomato paste, then stir in the hot stock and season generously. Cover and cook on Low for 5–6 hours, until the rice and beets are tender.

Stir the risotto, spoon onto plates, and top each portion with a spoonful of yogurt, some smoked salmon, and a few arugula leaves. Serve immediately.

For pumpkin & sage risotto, place 2 cups diced pumpkin in the slow cooker pot with 1 finely chopped white onion and 2 chopped garlic cloves. Mix in 1¼ cups rinsed brown rice and flavor with 2 sage sprigs, 1 teaspoon paprika, and 2 teaspoons tomato paste. Add 5 cups hot vegetable stock, season and cook as above. Serve sprinkled with ¾ cup finely grated Parmesan cheese. **Calories per serving 354**

cidered ham hotpot

Calories per serving **375**
Serves **4**
Preparation time **25 minutes**
Cooking time **6–7 hours**

1 lb **unsmoked ham joint**,
   trimmed of fat
1¼ lb **baking potatoes**, cut
   into ¾ inch chunks
7 oz small **shallots**, peeled
3 **carrots**, thickly sliced
2 **celery sticks**, thickly sliced
1 large **leek**, thickly sliced
2 **bay leaves**
¾ cup **hard cider**
¾ cup hot **chicken stock**
¼ teaspoon **cloves**
1 teaspoon **dry mustard**
pepper
3 tablespoons chopped
   chives, to garnish

Preheat the slow cooker if necessary. Rinse the ham joint with cold water and place in the slow cooker pot with the potatoes. Arrange the shallots, carrots, celery, and leek slices around the ham, then tuck in the bay leaves.

Pour the cider and stock into a saucepan, add the cloves and dry mustard, then season with pepper (ham joints can be salty so don't be tempted to add salt). Bring to a boil, then pour around the ham. Cover and cook on High for 6–7 hours, until the ham is cooked through.

Cut the ham into pieces and serve in shallow bowls with the vegetables and stock, garnished with chopped chives.

For ham in cola, follow the recipe above, using 1¾ cups diet cola instead of the cider and stock and omitting the potatoes. Serve with 1¼ lb boiled baby new potatoes and 1¾ cups steamed green beans. **Calories per serving 376**

vegetable moussaka

Calories per serving **322**
Serves **4**
Preparation time **25 minutes**
Cooking time **7–9½ hours**

low-calorie cooking oil spray
1 **onion**, coarsely chopped
1 large **eggplant**, sliced
2 **garlic cloves**, finely chopped
1 **red bell pepper**, cored,
　seeded, and cut into chunks
1 **yellow bell pepper**, cored,
　seeded, and cut into chunks
2 large **zucchini**, thickly sliced
2 cups **tomato puree** or
　tomato sauce
⅔ cup **vegetable stock**
⅓ cup **dried Puy lentils**
leaves from 3 **rosemary**
　sprigs, chopped
1 teaspoon **granular**
　sweetener
salt and **pepper**

Topping
1 cup **0% fat Greek yogurt**
3 **eggs**
¼ grated **Parmesan cheese**

Preheat the slow cooker if necessary. Spray a large skillet with a little low-calorie cooking oil spray and place over high heat until hot. Add the onion and eggplant and cook for 4–5 minutes, stirring until just beginning to brown. Add the garlic, peppers, and zucchini and cook for 2 minutes more, then add the tomato puree or sauce, stock and lentils.

Add the rosemary and sweetener and season to taste. Bring to a boil, stirring, then transfer to the slow cooker pot. Cover and cook on Low for 6–8 hours, until the lentils are tender.

Mix the yogurt, eggs, and a little pepper together in a bowl until smooth. Stir the vegetable mixture, then smooth the surface with the back of a spoon. Pour the yogurt mixture over the top in an even layer and sprinkle with the Parmesan. Cover and continue cooking for 45 minutes–1¼ hours until the custard has set.

Place the slow cooker pot under a preheated hot broiler for 4–5 minutes, until the top is golden, then serve with a green salad, if desired.

For penne with Mediterranean vegetables, make and cook the vegetable and lentil mixture as above. Cook 3¼ oz dried whole-wheat penne pasta in a saucepan of lightly salted boiling water according to package instructions. Drain and stir into the cooked vegetables, spoon into shallow dishes, and sprinkle with ¼ cup grated Parmesan cheese. **Calories per serving 399**

asian pork with bok choy

Calories per serving **387**
Serves **4**
Preparation time **20 minutes**
Cooking time **6¼–7¼ hours**

4 **pork tenderloin slices**,
 11½ oz in total
1 **red onion**, thinly sliced
1 inch piece of **fresh ginger
 root**, thinly sliced
1 **garlic clove**, thinly sliced
small handful of **fresh cilantro
 leaves**
¼ teaspoon **dried red pepper
 flakes**
2 small **star anise**
1 teaspoon **Thai fish sauce**
2 teaspoons **tomato paste**
4 teaspoons **dark soy sauce**
1½ cups hot **chicken stock**
7 oz **bok choy**, thickly sliced
3½ oz **asparagus tips**
8 oz **dried egg noodles**, to
 serve

Preheat the slow cooker if necessary. Place the pork tenderlions slices in the slow cooker pot in a single layer and sprinkle with the onion, ginger, and garlic. Sprinkle half the cilantro leaves on top.

Stir the pepper flakes, star anise, fish sauce, tomato paste, and soy sauce into the hot chicken stock, then pour over the pork. Cover and cook on Low for 6–7 hours, until the pork is tender.

Add the bok choy and asparagus to the slow cooker pot, cover, and cook on High for 15 minutes, until the vegetables are just tender and still bright green.

Meanwhile, cook the egg noodles in a saucepan of lightly salted boiling water according to package instructions until tender. Drain and divide among 4 bowls, top with the pork and vegetables, then spoon over the broth and serve garnished with the remaining cilantro.

For asian pork with mixed vegetables, follow the recipe above, adding 10 oz ready-prepared mixed stir-fry vegetables instead of the bok choy and asparagus. **Calories per serving 409**

shakshuka

Calories per serving **314**
Serves **4**
Preparation time **20 minutes**
Cooking time **3½–4½ hours**

low-calorie cooking oil spray
2 **red onions**, coarsely
  chopped
3 oz **chorizo**, diced
1¼ lb **tomatoes**, chopped
½ teaspoon **dried red pepper**
  flakes
1 tablespoon **tomato paste**
2 teaspoons **granular**
  sweetener
2 teaspoons **paprika**
1 teaspoon **dried oregano**
4 **eggs**
salt and **pepper**

To serve
chopped **parsley**
4 small slices of **whole-wheat**
  bread, toasted

Preheat the slow cooker if necessary. Spray a large skillet with a little low-calorie cooking oil spray and place over medium heat until hot. Add the onion and chorizo and cook for 5 minutes, stirring until the onion has softened.

Add the diced tomatoes, pepper flakes, tomato paste, sweetener, paprika, and oregano and season to taste. Transfer the mixture to the slow cooker pot, cover, and cook on High for 3–4 hours, until the tomatoes have softened and the sauce is thick.

Make 4 indents in the tomato mixture with the back of a dessert spoon, then break an egg into each one. Cover again and cook for 15 minutes or until the eggs are set to your liking. Sprinkle with a little chopped parsley, then spoon onto plates and serve with toast.

For mixed vegetable shakshuka, follow the recipe above, omitting the chorizo and using just 1 chopped red onion. Add 1 diced red bell pepper, 1 large diced zucchini, and 2 finely chopped garlic cloves to the skillet with the onion and continue as above. **Calories per serving 205**

beef bourguignon

Calories per serving **317 (not including rice)**
Serves **4**
Preparation time **20 minutes**
Cooking time **10–11 hours**

low-calorie cooking oil spray
1¼ lb **stewing beef**, trimmed of fat and cubed
3½ oz **bacon**, diced
10 oz small **shallots**, peeled
3 **garlic cloves**, finely chopped
1 tablespoon **all-purpose flour**
⅔ cup **red wine**
1¼ cups **beef stock**
1 tablespoon **tomato paste**
small bunch of **mixed herbs** or a **dried bouquet garni**
salt and **pepper**
chopped **parsley**, to garnish

Preheat the slow cooker if necessary. Spray a large skillet with a little low-calorie cooking oil spray and place over high heat until hot. Add the beef, a few pieces at a time until all the beef is in the pan, and cook for 5 minutes, stirring, until browned. Use a slotted spoon to transfer the beef to the slow cooker pot.

Add the bacon and shallots to the skillet and cook over medium heat for 2–3 minutes, until the bacon is just beginning to brown. Stir in the garlic and flour, then add the wine, stock, tomato paste, and herbs. Season to taste and bring to a boil, stirring.

Pour the sauce over the beef, cover, and cook on Low for 10–11 hours, until the beef is tender. Stir, garnish with chopped parsley, and serve with rice, if desired.

For beef goulash, follow the recipe above, adding 2 teaspoons mild paprika, 1 teaspoon caraway seeds, ¼ teaspoon ground cinnamon, and ¼ teaspoon ground allspice instead of the herbs. **Calories per serving 319**

slow-cooked greek lamb

Calories per serving **353**
Serves **4**
Preparation time **20 minutes**
Cooking time **9¼–10½ hours**

low-calorie cooking oil spray
4 **lean lamb leg steaks**,
   4 oz each
1 large **onion**, thinly sliced
2 **garlic cloves**, finely chopped
1 **lemon**, diced
1¼ cups coarsely chopped
   tomatoes
2 teaspoons **coriander seeds**,
   coarsely crushed
1 **bay leaf**
1 teaspoon **granular**
   sweetener
1 tablespoon **tomato paste**
1¼ cups **lamb stock**
10 oz **baby new potatoes**,
   thickly sliced
1¾ cups diced **zucchini**
salt and **pepper**
2 tablespoons chopped
   parsley, to garnish

Preheat the slow cooker if necessary. Spray a large skillet with a little low-calorie cooking oil spray and place over high heat until hot. Add the lamb steaks and cook for 4–5 minutes, turning once, until browned on both sides. Transfer to a plate.

Add the onion to the skillet and cook for 4–5 minutes, until softened, then add the garlic, lemon, and tomatoes. Add the coriander seeds, bay leaf, sweetener, tomato paste, and lamb stock, season to taste and bring to a boil.

Arrange the potatoes over the bottom of the slow cooker pot, then place the lamb steaks in a single layer on top. Pour over the hot stock mixture, cover, and cook on Low for 9–10 hours, until the lamb and potatoes are tender.

Add the zucchini, cover again, and cook on High for 15–30 minutes, until tender. Spoon into shallow bowls, sprinkle with the parsley, and serve immediately.

For slow-cooked lamb with rosemary, follow the recipe above, adding 3 rosemary sprigs instead of the lemon, cilantro seeds, and bay leaf. Cook as above, adding the zucchini at the end. Serve garnished with the parsley. **Calories per serving 352**

tarragon chicken with mushrooms

Calories per serving **319**
Serves **4**
Preparation time **20 minutes**
Cooking time **8¼–9½ hours**

low-calorie cooking oil spray
4 skinless **chicken legs**,
  2 lb 6 oz in total
2 **leeks**, sliced
2¼ cups sliced **closed-cap
  mushrooms**
1 tablespoon **all-purpose
  flour**
1 teaspoon **dry mustard**
2 cups **chicken stock**
2 tablespoons chopped
  tarragon, plus extra to
  garnish
3 tablespoons **sherry**
  (optional)
1 cup **green beans**
salt and **pepper**

Preheat the slow cooker if necessary. Spray a large skillet with a little low-calorie cooking oil spray and place over high heat until hot. Add the chicken legs and cook for 4–5 minutes, turning once, until golden. Transfer to the slow cooker pot.

Add a little extra low-calorie cooking oil spray to the pan if necessary, then add the white leek slices (reserving the green slices) and the mushrooms and cook for 2–3 minutes. Stir in the flour, then add the dry mustard, stock, tarragon, and sherry, if using. Season to taste and bring to a boil, stirring.

Pour the liquid and vegetables over the chicken, cover, and cook on Low for 8–9 hours, until the chicken is tender and cooked through.

Stir the casserole, then add the remaining green leek slices and the green beans. Cover again and cook on High for 15–30 minutes, until the vegetables are tender. Spoon into shallow bowls and serve garnished with a little extra tarragon.

For low-cal garlicky mash, to serve as an accompaniment, peel and cut 1¼ lb potatoes into chunks and cook in a saucepan of lightly salted boiling water for about 15 minutes, until tender. Drain and mash with 3 tablespoons chicken stock, 2 crushed garlic cloves, and a little salt and pepper. **Calories per serving 122**

venison sausages with red cabbage

Calories per serving **354**
Serves **4**
Preparation time **20 minutes**
Cooking time **5–6 hours**

8 **venison sausages**,
   1 lb 1 oz in total
low-calorie cooking oil spray
1 **onion**, chopped
²/₃ cup **red wine**
2½ cups **beef stock**
2 tablespoons **cranberry
   sauce**
1 tablespoon **tomato paste**
2 **bay leaves**
10 oz **potatoes**, cut into 1 inch
   chunks
2 **carrots**, cut into ¾ inch
   chunks
1¼ cups coarsely chopped
   tomatoes
2 cups finely shredded **red
   cabbage**
½ cup **dried green lentils**
salt and **pepper**

Preheat the slow cooker if necessary. Cook the sausages under a preheated medium broiler for 5 minutes, turning until browned but not cooked through.

Meanwhile, spray a large skillet with a little low-calorie cooking oil spray and place over medium heat until hot. Add the onion and cook for 4–5 minutes, until just softened. Add the red wine, stock, cranberry sauce, tomato paste, and bay leaves, then season with salt and pepper to taste and bring to a boil, stirring.

Place the potatoes and carrots in the slow cooker pot with the tomatoes, red cabbage, and lentils on top. Pour over the hot wine mixture, then add the sausages and press down into the liquid. Cover and cook on High for 5–6 hours, until the sausages and potatoes are cooked through and the lentils are tender. Serve in shallow bowls.

For braised lamb shanks with red cabbage, omit the venison sausages and brown 4 small lamb shanks, 1½ lb in total, in a little low-calorie cooking oil spray in a skillet, then continue with the recipe above. **Calories per serving 335**

138

mushroom & wheat berry pilau

Calories per serving **316**
Serves **4**
Preparation time **20 minutes**
Cooking time **3½–4 hours**

1 tablespoon **olive oil**
1 **onion**, thinly sliced
2 **garlic cloves**, finely chopped
1⅓ cups **brown ale**
2 cups **vegetable stock**
3 **sage sprigs**
¼ teaspoon grated **nutmeg**
2 inch **cinnamon stick**
1 tablespoon **tomato paste**
1 cup **wheat berries**
8 oz **cremini mushrooms**, halved
8 oz large **closed-cap mushrooms**, quartered
salt and **pepper**
¼ cup **parsley**, coarsely chopped, to garnish

Preheat the slow cooker if necessary. Heat the oil in a large skillet over a medium heat until hot. Add the onion and fry for 4–5 minutes, stirring until just beginning to soften. Add the garlic, brown ale, stock, sage, nutmeg, and cinnamon. Stir in the tomato paste and season well, then bring to a boil.

Place the wheat berries and mushrooms in the slow cooker pot. Pour over the hot ale mixture, then cover and cook on High for 3½–4 hours, until the wheat berries are tender and nearly all the liquid has been absorbed. Stir well, then sprinkle with the parsley. Spoon into shallow bowls to serve.

For red pepper wheat berry pilau, cook 1 sliced red onion in the oil as above, then add 2 finely chopped garlic cloves and 2 cored, seeded, and sliced red bell peppers. Stir in ¾ cup red wine, 2½ cups vegetable stock, a small handful of basil leaves, and 1 tablespoon tomato paste. Season to taste and bring to a boil, then pour over the wheatberries in the slow cooker pot and cook as above. **Calories per serving 363**

three-fish gratin

Calories per serving **395**
Serves **4**
Preparation time **20 minutes**
Cooking time **2¼–3¼ hours**

2 tablespoons **cornstarch**
1⅔ cups **skim milk**
½ cup shredded **sharp cheddar cheese**
3 tablespoons chopped **parsley**
1 **leek**, thinly sliced
1 **bay leaf**
1 lb **mixed fish**, diced (such as salmon, cod, and smoked haddock)
salt and **pepper**

Topping
½ cup **fresh bread crumbs**
⅓ cup shredded **sharp cheddar cheese**

To serve
2 cups **peas**
3 cups **snow peas**, steamed

Preheat the slow cooker if necessary. Place the cornstarch in a saucepan with a little of the milk and mix to a smooth paste. Stir in the rest of the milk, then add the cheese, parsley, leek, and bay leaf. Season to taste and bring to a boil, stirring until thickened.

Place the fish in the slow cooker pot. Pour over the hot leek sauce, cover, and cook on Low for 2–3 hours, until the fish is cooked through.

Transfer the fish mixture to a shallow ovenproof dish, sprinkle the bread crumbs and cheese over the top, then place under a preheated hot broiler for 4–5 minutes until golden brown. Serve with the steamed peas and snow peas.

For fish pies, follow the recipe above, omitting the bread crumb and cheese topping. Peel and cut ¼ lb potatoes into chunks. Cook the potatoes in a saucepan of lightly salted boiling water for 15 minutes or until tender. Drain and mash with ¼ cup skim milk, then season and stir in ⅓ cup shredded sharp cheddar cheese. Divide the cooked fish mixture among 4 individual pie dishes, spoon over the mash, rough up the top with a fork, then brush with 1 beaten egg. Cook under a preheated medium broiler until golden. **Calories per serving 435**

thai fish curry

Calories per serving **326**
Serves **4**
Preparation time **15 minutes**
Cooking time **2¼–3¼ hours**

1 **onion**, quartered
½ cup **fresh cilantro leaves**
  and **stems**, plus extra to
  garnish
1 inch piece of **fresh ginger
  root**, sliced
1 **lemon grass stalk**, thickly
  sliced, or 1 teaspoon **lemon
  grass paste**
¾ cup **light coconut milk**
¾ cup **fish stock**
1 teaspoon **Thai fish sauce**
1 tablespoon **Thai red curry
  paste**
4 **salmon steaks**, 1 lb in total
low-calorie cooking oil spray
13 oz **ready-prepared stir-fry
  vegetables**
grated zest and juice of 1 **lime**

Preheat the slow cooker if necessary. Place the onion, cilantro, ginger, and lemon grass in a food processor and blitz until finely chopped. Transfer to a medium saucepan and stir in the coconut milk, stock, fish sauce, and curry paste. This mixture can be chilled until ready to use.

Arrange the salmon steaks in the bottom of the slow cooker pot. Bring the coconut mixture to a boil, stirring, then pour over the salmon. Cover and cook on Low for 2–3 hours, until the salmon flakes easily when pressed with a small knife.

Spray a large skillet with a little low-calorie cooking oil spray and place over high heat until hot. Add the vegetables and cook for 2–3 minutes, until piping hot.

Break the salmon into large flakes and stir the lime zest and juice into the curry. Spoon into bowls and top with the vegetables and a little extra cilantro.

For Thai vegetable curry, follow the recipe above to make the sauce, using ¾ cup vegetable stock instead of the fish stock, and omitting the fish sauce if serving the curry to vegetarians. Place 1½ cups canned bamboo shoots in the slow cooker pot with 1 cup baby corn, ¾ cup whole cherry tomatoes, and 1 diced zucchini. Pour over the sauce, cook and serve with stir-fried vegetables as above. **Calories per serving 138**

tangy turkey tagine

Calories per serving **385**
  (not including naan)
Serves **4**
Preparation time **25 minutes**
Cooking time **8–9 hours**

low-calorie cooking oil spray
13 oz **turkey breast**, diced
1 **onion**, chopped
2 **garlic cloves**, finely chopped
1 tablespoon **all-purpose**
  flour
2 cups **chicken stock**
2 pinches of **saffron strands**
  or 1 teaspoon **ground**
  turmeric
2 inch **cinnamon stick**
finely grated zest of 1 **lemon**
13 oz can **chickpeas**, drained
3 tablespoons **golden raisins**
salt and **pepper**

To serve
1 cup **couscous**
2 cups boiling **water**
¼ cup chopped **mint** or mixed
  mint and **parsley**

Preheat the slow cooker if necessary. Spray a large skillet with a little low-calorie cooking oil spray and place over high heat until hot. Add the turkey, a few pieces at a time until all the turkey is in the pan, and cook for 5 minutes, stirring until golden. Use a slotted spoon to transfer the turkey to a plate.

Add the onion to the skillet and cook for 4–5 minutes, until softened. Stir in the garlic and flour, then add the stock and mix well. Add the saffron or turmeric, cinnamon, and lemon zest, then the chickpeas, and golden raisins. Season to taste and bring to a boil, stirring.

Pour into the slow cooker pot, add the turkey pieces and press into the liquid. Cover and cook on Low for 8–9 hours, until the turkey is tender and cooked through.

Meanwhile, place the couscous in a mixing bowl, pour over a boiling water, cover with a plate and let soak for 5 minutes, until tender. Stir in the chopped herbs, season to taste and fluff up with a fork. Divide the couscous among 4 plates and top with the tagine. Serve with naan, if desired.

For harissa-baked turkey, follow the recipe above, using 1¼ cups chicken stock and 1¼ cups diced tomatoes instead of 2 cups chicken stock. Omit the saffron, cinnamon and lemon and add 2 teaspoons harissa paste and 1 inch piece of fresh ginger root, chopped, instead. Cook as above and serve with the herby couscous. **Calories per serving 396**

beery beef cheeks

Calories per serving **363**
Serves **4**
Preparation time **20 minutes**
Cooking time **5–6 hours**

1 tablespoon **sunflower oil**
1¼ lb **beef cheeks**, cut into
   1½ inch thick slices
2 **red onions**, cut into wedges
1 cup **brown ale**
⅔ cup **beef stock**
1 tablespoon **tomato paste**
2 teaspoons **cornstarch**
2 **rosemary sprigs**
2 **bay leaves**
10 oz small **Chantenay
   carrots**, halved lengthwise
2 **celery sticks**, thickly sliced
salt and **pepper**

Heat the oil in a large skillet over high heat until hot. Add the beef, a few pieces at a time until all the beef is in the pan, and cook for 5 minutes, stirring until browned. Use a slotted spoon to transfer the beef to the slow cooker pot, arranging it in a single layer.

Add the onion to the skillet and cook for 3–4 minutes, until softened. Add the brown ale, stock, and tomato paste. Mix the cornstarch to a smooth paste with a little cold water and stir into the pan with the herbs. Season to taste and bring to a boil, stirring.

Place the carrots and celery on top of the beef, then pour over the hot beer mixture. Cover and cook on High for 5–6 hours, until the beef is very tender. Spoon into shallow bowls and serve with sugar snap peas and frozen peas, if desired.

For beery chestnuts & mushrooms, follow the recipe above, using 1 lb whole mixed small mushrooms instead of the beef, and adding 1½ cups canned chestnuts at the same time as the herbs. **Calories per serving 219**

pork stew with sweet potatoes

Calories per serving **315**
Serves **4**
Preparation time **20 minutes**
Cooking time **8¼–9¼ hours**

low-calorie cooking oil spray

1 lb **lean pork**, cubed

1 **onion**, chopped

1½ cups sliced **closed-cap mushrooms**

2 cups **chicken stock**

2 tablespoons **tomato paste**

2 tablespoons **soy sauce**

¼ teaspoon **chili powder**

½ teaspoon **ground allspice**

¼ teaspoon **ground cinnamon**

1 teaspoon **granular sweetener**

1 cup thinly sliced **carrots**

2 **celery sticks**, thickly sliced

12 oz **sweet potato**, cut into 1 inch chunks

1 cup shredded **curly kale**

Preheat the slow cooker if necessary. Spray a large skillet with a little low-calorie cooking oil spray and place over high heat until hot. Add the pork, a few pieces at a time until all the pork is in the pan, and cook for 3 minutes, stirring. Add the onion and cook for another 2–3 minutes, until the pork is golden.

Stir in the mushrooms, then add the stock, tomato paste and soy sauce. Add the chili powder, allspice, cinnamon, and sweetener, season to taste and bring to a boil, stirring.

Place the carrots, celery, and sweet potato in the slow cooker pot, then pour over the pork and sauce. Press the meat into the liquid, cover, and cook on Low for 8–9 hours, until the pork is tender.

Stir the stew, then add the kale. Cover again and cook on High for 15 minutes, then spoon into bowls and serve immediately.

For fragrant sausage & sweet potato stew, place 1 lb reduced-fat pork sausages under a preheated hot broiler until browned but not cooked through. Transfer to the slow cooker pot. Continue with the recipe above, omitting the pork. **Calories per serving 362**

polish sausage stew

Calories per serving **355**
Serves **4**
Preparation time **20 minutes**
Cooking time **8–10 hours**

low-calorie cooking oil spray
11 oz boneless, skinless
  chicken thighs, cubed
1 **onion**, chopped
2 teaspoons **mild paprika**
1 teaspoon **caraway seeds**
1 **dessert apple**, quartered,
  cored, and thinly sliced
1 cup diced **tomatoes**
1 tablespoon **granular**
  sweetener
2 cups **sauerkraut**, drained
7 oz **smoked pork sausage**,
  sliced
3½ oz **gherkins**, sliced
2 cups hot **chicken stock**
salt and **pepper**

To garnish
3 tablespoons chopped
  dill weed
3 tablespoons chopped
  parsley

Preheat the slow cooker if necessary. Spray a large skillet with a little low-calorie cooking oil spray and place over high heat until hot. Add the chicken, a few pieces at a time until all the chicken is in the pan, then add the onion and cook for 5 minutes, stirring, until the chicken is golden.

Add the paprika, caraway, apple, tomatoes, and sweetener to the pan and heat through. Place the sauerkraut in the slow cooker pot and pour the chicken mixture on top, then add the sliced sausage and gherkins.

Pour over the hot stock and season to taste. Stir well, cover, and cook on Low for 8–10 hours, until the chicken is cooked through. Serve in bowls, garnished with chopped dill and parsley.

For Polish pork stew, follow the recipe above, using 1 lb diced lean pork instead of the chicken. Use 1 teaspoon mild paprika and 1 teaspoon smoked hot paprika or chili powder instead of 2 teaspoons mild paprika, and continue with the recipe, omitting the smoked sausage. **Calories per serving 251**

skinny cassoulet

Calories per serving **364**
Serves **4**
Preparation time **20 minutes**
Cooking time **8–10 hours**

low-calorie cooking oil spray
1 lb **lean pork**, diced
3 oz **chorizo**, sliced
1 **onion**, chopped
3 **garlic cloves**, finely chopped
1 **red bell pepper**, cored,
  seeded, and diced
2 **celery sticks**, sliced
1 **carrot**, diced
2 cups **tomato puree** or
  tomato sauce
1 teaspoon **dried**
  Mediterranean herbs
2 x 15 oz cans **cannellini**
  beans, drained
3 tablespoons **fresh**
  bread crumbs
salt and **pepper**

Preheat the slow cooker if necessary. Spray a large skillet with a little low-calorie cooking oil spray and place over high heat until hot. Add the pork, a few pieces at a time until all the pork is in the pan, and cook for 5 minutes, stirring, until browned. Use a slotted spoon to transfer the pork to the slow cooker pot.

Add the chorizo and onion to the skillet and cook for 4–5 minutes, until the onion has softened. Stir in the garlic, red pepper, celery, carrot, tomato puree or sauce, and herbs. Season to taste and bring to a boil, stirring.

Place the beans in the slow cooker pot, pour over the tomato mixture and stir well. Level the surface with the back of a spoon, then sprinkle over the bread crumbs. Cover and cook on Low for 8–10 hours, until the pork is tender. Spoon into shallow bowls and serve with salad, if desired.

For chicken cassoulet, follow the recipe above, using 1 lb boneless, skinless chicken thighs, diced, instead of the pork. Mix the bread crumbs with 2 tablespoons chopped rosemary and 2 tablespoons chopped parsley, then spoon over the cassoulet and cook as above.
Calories per serving 346

feijoada ham

Calories per serving **312**
Serves **4**
Preparation time **20 minutes**
Cooking time **5–6 hours**

1 **onion**, chopped
2 **celery sticks**, thickly sliced
1 cup diced **carrots**
15 oz can **black beans**,
 drained
1 **red chile**, halved and
 seeded
2 **thyme sprigs**
pared peel of 1 **orange**
1 lb **unsmoked ham joint**,
 trimmed of fat
1 teaspoon **mild paprika**
½ teaspoon **ground allspice**
2 cups hot **vegetable stock**
salt and **pepper**
¼ cup chopped **parsley**,
 to garnish

To serve
¾ cup **rice**

Preheat the slow cooker if necessary. Place the onion, celery, and carrot in the slow cooker pot, then add the drained beans, chile, thyme, and orange peel. Nestle the ham joint in the center.

Stir the paprika and allspice into the hot stock, then season to taste and pour over the ham joint. Spoon some of the orange peel and thyme on top of the joint, cover, and cook on High for 5–6 hours, until the ham is very tender.

Cook the rice in a saucepan of lightly salted boiling water, according to package instructions, until tender.

Cut the ham into pieces, then spoon into shallow bowls with the beans, vegetables, and sauce. Sprinkle with the parsley and serve with the rice.

For feijoada chicken, follow the recipe above, using a 2 lb 10 oz oven-ready chicken instead of the ham joint. Cook on High for 5–6 hours or until the chicken is thoroughly cooked and the meat juices run clear when the thickest parts of the leg and breast are pierced with a sharp knife. **Calories per serving 318**

salmon bourride

Calories per serving **336**
Serves **4**
Preparation time **20 minutes**
Cooking time **3–3½ hours**

low-calorie cooking oil spray
1 **onion**, chopped
2 **garlic cloves**, finely chopped
½ **red bell pepper**, cored,
   seeded, and very thinly sliced
½ **orange bell pepper**, cored,
   seeded, and very thinly sliced
14½ oz can **diced tomatoes**
⅓ cup **vegetable stock**
1 teaspoon **granular
   sweetener**
1 teaspoon **cornstarch**
14 oz can **artichoke hearts**,
   drained
4 **salmon steaks**, 4½ oz each
finely grated zest of 1 **lemon**
½ teaspoon **dried
   Mediterranean herbs**
salt and **pepper**
2 cups steamed **green beans**,
   to serve

Preheat the slow cooker if necessary. Spray a large skillet with a little low-calorie cooking oil spray and place over high heat until hot. Add the onion, garlic, and peppers and cook for 4–5 minutes, until softened.

Stir in the tomatoes, stock, and sweetener. Mix the cornstarch to a smooth paste with a little cold water and stir into the pan. Season with salt and pepper to taste and bring to a boil, stirring.

Transfer the mixture into the slow cooker pot, stir in the artichoke hearts, then arrange the salmon steaks in a single layer on top, pressing them down into the liquid. Sprinkle the lemon zest and herbs over the salmon and season lightly.

Cover and cook on Low for 3–3½ hours, until the salmon steaks are cooked and flake easily when pressed with a small knife. Spoon into shallow bowls and serve with the steamed green beans.

For squid bourride, rinse 1¼ lb prepared squid and take the tentacles out of the tubes. Slice the squid tubes and drain well. Follow the recipe above, using the sliced squid tubes instead of the salmon and cooking on Low for 4–5 hours. Add the squid tentacles and continue cooking for 30 minutes, until tender, then serve with the steamed green beans. **Calories per serving 205**

tangy chicken, fennel & leek braise

Calories per serving **316**
Serves **4**
Preparation time **20 minutes**
Cooking time **8½–9½ hours**

low-calorie cooking oil spray
1¼ lb boneless, skinless
   chicken thighs, halved
1 **fennel bulb**, cored and
   sliced, green fronds reserved
2 **leeks**, thinly sliced
1½ cups **chicken stock**
finely grated zest and juice of
   ½ **orange**
2 teaspoons **cornstarch**
salt and **pepper**

Preheat the slow cooker if necessary. Spray a large skillet with a little low-calorie cooking oil spray and place over high heat until hot. Add the chicken and cook for 3–4 minutes, turning once, until browned on both sides. Use a slotted spoon to transfer to a plate.

Add the fennel and white leek slices to the skillet, reserving the green slices. Cook for 2–3 minutes, until just beginning to soften, then add the stock, and orange zest and juice. Mix the cornstarch to a smooth paste with a little cold water and stir into the pan. Season to taste and bring to a boil, stirring.

Transfer the mixture to the slow cooker pot, arrange the chicken pieces on top in a single layer and press into the liquid. Cover and cook on Low for 8–9 hours, until the chicken is cooked through.

Add the reserved green leek slices, stir into the sauce, cover again and cook for 30 minutes. Serve garnished with the reserved fennel fronds.

For braised mustard chicken & leeks, follow the recipe above, using 3 oz diced lean Canadian bacon instead of the fennel. Use 1 teaspoon Dijon mustard instead of the orange zest and juice and cook as above. Garnish with chopped parsley.
Calories per serving 323

vegetarian sausages & onions

Calories per serving **374**
Serves **4**
Preparation time **20 minutes**
Cooking time **4½–5½ hours**

low-calorie cooking oil spray
15 oz **soy sausages**
1 cup thinly sliced **onions**
2 teaspoons **dark brown sugar**
1½ cups **vegetable stock**
1 tablespoon **tomato paste**
2 teaspoons **whole-grain mustard**
2 teaspoons **cornstarch**
salt and **pepper**
1 lb 6 oz **celeriac**, cubed just before cooking
chopped **parsley**, to garnish (optional)

To serve
3 cups **green beans**, steamed

Preheat the slow cooker if necessary. Spray a large skillet with a little low-calorie cooking oil spray and place over high heat until hot. Add the sausages and cook for 2–3 minutes until browned all over. Transfer to the slow cooker pot in a single layer.

Add a little extra low-calorie cooking oil spray to the skillet, add the onions and cook over medium heat for 5 minutes until just beginning to soften. Add the sugar and continue to cook for 5 minutes until deep brown, being careful not to burn the onions.

Stir in the stock, tomato paste and mustard. Mix the cornstarch to a smooth paste with a little cold water and stir into the pan. Season to taste and bring to a boil, stirring. Pour over the sausages, cover, and cook on High for 4–5 hours until the sausages are cooked through.

Cook the celeriac in a saucepan of lightly salted boiling water for 15–20 minutes until tender. Drain and mash the celeriac with 3–4 tablespoons of the cooking water and season to taste. Divide the mash between 4 serving plates and top with the sausages and onion gravy. Sprinkle with a little chopped parsley, if desired, and serve with the steamed green beans.

For pork sausages & onions, broil 8 reduced-fat pork sausages until browned all over but not cooked through and arrange in the slow cooker pot. Follow the recipe above to make the onion gravy, pour over the sausages and cook on High for 5–6 hours, until the sausages are cooked through. Serve with celeriac mash and green beans, as above. **Calories per serving 351**

red pepper & chorizo tortilla

Calories per serving **309**
Serves **4**
Preparation time **20 minutes**
Cooking time **2–2½ hours**

1 tablespoon **olive oil**, plus
   extra for greasing
1 small **onion**, chopped
3 oz **chorizo**, diced
6 **eggs**
⅔ cup **milk**
1 cup **roasted red peppers**
   from a jar, sliced
8 oz cooked **potatoes**, sliced
salt and **pepper**

Preheat the slow cooker if necessary. Lightly oil a 5 cup ovenproof soufflé dish and line the bottom with nonstick parchment paper. Heat the oil in a small skillet over medium heat, add the onion and chorizo and cook for 4–5 minutes, until the onion has softened.

Beat the eggs and milk together in a mixing bowl and season with salt and pepper to taste. Add the onion and chorizo, red peppers, and potatoes and toss together.

Pour the mixture into the oiled dish, cover the top with foil, and put in the slow cooker pot. Pour boiling water into the slow cooker pot to come halfway up the sides of the dish, cover, and cook on High for 2–2½ hours until the egg mixture has just set in the center.

Loosen the edges of the tortilla with a round-bladed knife, turn it out onto a plate and peel off the lining paper. Cut into slices and serve hot or cold, with salad if desired.

For cheesy bacon & rosemary tortilla, follow the recipe above, using 3 oz diced smoked bacon instead of the chorizo. Beat the eggs and milk in a bowl with the chopped leaves from 2 small rosemary sprigs, ¼ cup freshly grated Parmesan or cheddar cheese and ⅓ cup sliced button mushrooms. Season to taste and continue as above. **Calories per serving 282**

smoked cod with bean mash

Calories per serving **308**
Serves **4**
Preparation time **20 minutes**
Cooking time **1½–2 hours**

2 x 15 oz cans **cannellini beans**, drained
bunch of **scallions**, thinly sliced
1⅔ cups hot **fish stock**
1 teaspoon **whole-grain mustard**
grated zest and juice of 1 **lemon**
4 **smoked cod loins**, 1¼ lb in total
¼ cup **crème fraîche** or **sour cream**
small bunch of **parsley**, **watercress** or **arugula leaves**, coarsely chopped
salt and **pepper**

Preheat the slow cooker if necessary. Put the beans into the slow cooker pot with the white scallion slices (reserving the green slices). Mix the fish stock with the mustard and lemon zest and juice, season to taste and pour into the pot.

Arrange the fish on top and sprinkle with a little extra pepper. Cover and cook on Low for 1½–2 hours or until the fish flakes easily when pressed with a small knife. Transfer the fish to a plate and keep warm.

Pour off nearly all the cooking liquid, then mash the beans coarsely. Stir in the crème fraîche, the reserved green scallion slices, and the parsley, watercress, or arugula. Adjust the seasoning if necessary, spoon the mash onto 4 plates and top with the fish. Serve immediately.

For baked salmon with basil bean mash, follow the recipe above, omitting the mustard. Use 4 x 5 oz salmon steaks instead of the cod and a small bunch of basil instead of the parsley, watercress, or arugula leaves. **Calories per serving 451**

mushroom & tomato rigatoni

Calories per serving **385 (not
  including Parmesan)**
Serves **4**
Preparation time **20 minutes,
  plus soaking**
Cooking time **2½–3 hours**

8 oz **rigatoni** or **pasta quills**
3 tablespoons **olive oil**
1 **onion**, sliced
2–3 **garlic cloves**, finely
  chopped
1 cup sliced **closed-cap
  mushrooms**
8 oz **portabello mushrooms**,
  sliced
8 oz **tomatoes**, cut into
  chunks
14½ oz can **diced tomatoes**
¾ cup **vegetable stock**
1 tablespoon **tomato paste**
3 **rosemary sprigs**
salt and **pepper**

Preheat the slow cooker if necessary. Place the pasta
in a large bowl, cover with boiling water and let stand for
10 minutes.

Heat 1 tablespoon of the oil in a large skillet over
medium heat, add the onion, and cook for 5 minutes,
until softened. Stir in the remaining oil, the garlic, and
mushrooms and cook, stirring, until the mushrooms are
just beginning to brown.

Stir in the fresh and canned tomatoes, stock, and
tomato paste. Add the rosemary, season to taste, and
bring to a boil.

Drain the pasta and put it in the slow cooker pot. Pour
over the hot mushroom mixture and spread into an even
layer. Cover and cook on Low for 2½–3 hours or until
the pasta is just tender. Spoon into shallow bowls. Serve
sprinkled with Parmesan cheese, if desired.

For mushroom pastichio, follow the recipe above,
using 8 oz macaroni instead of the rigatoni. Mix 3 eggs
with 1 cup plain yogurt, 3 oz grated feta cheese, and a
pinch of grated nutmeg. Spoon the mixture over the top
of the mushroom and pasta mixture for the last hour of
cooking until set. Place under a preheated hot broiler to
brown the top before serving.
Calories per serving 416

tomato & squash curry

Calories per serving **308 (not including rice)**
Serves **4**
Preparation time **20 minutes**
Cooking time **5–6 hours**

2 tablespoons **butter**
1 **onion**, chopped
2⅔ cups peeled and diced **butternut squash**
2 **garlic cloves**, finely chopped
1½ inch piece of **fresh ginger root**, finely chopped
½–1 **mild red chile**, seeded and finely chopped
¼ cup prepared **korma curry paste**
⅔ cup **vegetable stock**
1¼ lb **plum tomatoes**, halved
2 oz **creamed coconut**, crumbled
salt and **pepper**
coarsely chopped **fresh cilantro**, to garnish

Preheat the slow cooker if necessary. Heat the butter in a large skillet over medium heat, add the onion and cook for 5 minutes, until softened. Stir in the butternut squash, garlic, ginger, and chile, to taste, and cook for 2–3 minutes. Mix in the curry paste and cook for 1 minute, then stir in the stock and bring to a boil.

Transfer the mixture to the slow cooker pot, then arrange the tomatoes, cut sides up, in a single layer on top. Sprinkle with the coconut and season to taste. Cover and cook on Low for 5–6 hours or until the squash is tender and the tomatoes are soft but still holding their shape.

Spoon into bowls, sprinkle with coarsely chopped cilantro and serve with pilau rice, if desired.

For quick pilau rice, to serve as an accompaniment, rinse ¾ cup basmati rice under cold running water, then drain. Heat 4 tablespoons butter and 1 tablespoon sunflower oil in a large skillet, add 1 chopped onion and cook until softened. Stir in 1 dried red chile, 1 cinnamon stick, halved, 1 teaspoon cumin seeds, 1 bay leaf, 6 crushed cardamom pods, ½ teaspoon ground turmeric, and a little salt. Add 2 cups boiling water, cover and simmer gently for 10 minutes. Take off the heat and let stand for 5–8 minutes without lifting the lid. Fluff up with a fork before serving. **Calories per serving 189**

eve's pudding

Calories per serving **335**
Serves **4**
Preparation time **25 minutes**
Cooking time **3–3½ hours**

4 tablespoons **sunflower margarine**, plus extra for greasing
¼ cup **granulated sugar**
6 tablespoons **all-purpose flour**
¼ cup **ground almonds**
¾ teaspoon **baking powder**
1 **egg**
grated zest and juice of 1 **lemon**
1 **dessert apple**, quartered, cored and sliced
1 tablespoon **apricot jelly**
¾ cup **instant powdered custard with sweetener**, to serve

Preheat the slow cooker if necessary. Grease the bottom and sides of a 6 inch round ovenproof dish, about 2½ inches deep, with a little margarine. Place the margarine, sugar, flour, almonds, and baking powder in a food processor, add the egg and lemon zest, and blend until smooth. Spoon into the dish and spread level.

Toss the apple slices with the lemon juice, then overlap in a ring on top of the pudding mixture. Cover the dish with greased foil and put in the slow cooker pot. Pour boiling water into the slow cooker pot to come halfway up the sides of the dish, cover, and cook on High for 3–3½ hours, until a knife comes out cleanly when inserted into the center.

Dot the top of the pudding with the apricot jelly, then gently spread into an even layer. Place under a preheated hot broiler for 3–4 minutes, until the top is lightly caramelized. Make the custard with boiling water according to package instructions and serve with the pudding.

For chocolate & pear pudding, follow the recipe above to make the pudding base, using 1 tablespoon unsweetened cocoa powder instead of the lemon zest. Quarter, core, and slice 1 small pear, toss with the lemon juice, then arrange over the pudding mixture. Cover and bake as above, then dust the top with a little sifted confectioners' sugar before serving.
Calories per serving 265

honeyed rice pudding

Calories per serving **366 (not including cream)**
Serves **4**
Preparation time **10 minutes**
Cooking time **2½–3 hours**

butter, for greasing
3 cups **whole milk**
3 tablespoons **honey**
½ cup **risotto rice**

Preheat the slow cooker if necessary. Lightly butter the inside of the slow cooker pot. Pour the milk into a saucepan, add the honey and bring just to a boil, stirring until the honey has melted. Pour into the slow cooker pot, add the rice, and stir gently.

Cover with the lid and cook on low for 2½–3 hours, stirring once during cooking, or until the pudding is thickened and the rice is soft. Stir again just before spooning into dishes. Top each bowl with 1 tablespoon of jelly and heavy cream, if desired.

For vanilla rice pudding, pour the milk into a saucepan, replace the honey with 3 tablespoons granulated sugar and bring just to a boil. Slit a vanilla bean, scrape the black seeds out with a small knife, and add to the milk with the pod. Pour into the greased slow cooker pot, add the rice and cook as above. Remove the vanilla pod before serving with heavy cream. **Calories per serving 364 (not including cream)**

blueberry & passion fruit cheesecake

Calories per serving **327**

Serves **4**

Preparation time **25 minutes, plus cooling and chilling**

Cooking time **2–2½ hours**

1 tablespoon **sunflower margarine**, plus extra for greasing

1 cup finely crushed **reduced-fat digestive biscuits**

1¼ cups **extra-light cream cheese**

¾ cup **0% fat Greek yogurt**

1 tablespoon **cornstarch**

finely grated zest and juice of ½ **lime**

1 teaspoon **vanilla extract**

3 tablespoons **granular sweetener**

3 tablespoons **granulated sugar**

2 **eggs**

1 cup **blueberries**

2 **passion fruits**, halved

Preheat the slow cooker if necessary. Grease the bottom and sides of a 6 inch round ovenproof dish, about 2½ inches deep, with a little margarine. Line the base with nonstick parchment paper.

Melt the margarine in a small saucepan and stir in the crushed crackers. Spoon into the dish and press down firmly to make a thin, even layer. Place the cheese, yogurt, and cornstarch in a mixing bowl and whisk until smooth. Add the lime zest and juice, vanilla, sweetener, sugar, and eggs and whisk again until smooth.

Pour the mixture into the dish and smooth the surface. Cover with greased foil and put in the slow cooker pot. Pour boiling water into the slow cooker pot to come halfway up the sides of the dish, cover, and cook on High for 2–2½ hours or until the cheesecake is set but with a slight wobble in the center. Remove from the slow cooker and let cool, then chill in the refrigerator for 3–4 hours or overnight.

Loosen the edge of the cheesecake with a knife, turn out of the dish and peel away the lining paper. Place on a serving plate, pile the blueberries on top, then scoop the passion fruit seeds over them. Serve cut into wedges.

For summer berry cheesecake, follow the recipe above to make the cheesecake, using the grated zest and juice of ½ lemon instead of the lime. Gently toss 1 cup sliced strawberries and 1 cup raspberries with 2 tablespoons reduced-sugar strawberry jelly and 1 tablespoon lemon juice instead of the blueberries and passion fruits. Turn out the cheesecake and top with the berry mixture just before serving. **Calories per serving 345**

recipes
under 500
calories

balsamic beef hotpot

Calories per serving **408**
Serves **4**
Preparation time **30 minutes**
Cooking time **7¼–8¼ hours**

low-calorie cooking oil spray
1 lb **lean stewing beef**,
   trimmed of fat and cubed
1 **onion**, chopped
8 oz **rutabaga**, cut into
   ¾ inch cubes
2 cups sliced **carrots**
¾ cup sliced **mushrooms**
2 teaspoons **all-purpose flour**
2 cups **beef stock**
2 tablespoons **balsamic
   vinegar**
1 teaspoon **dry mustard**
1 lb **potatoes**, sliced
salt and **pepper**
1 tablespoon chopped
   parsley, to garnish

To serve
1 cup **broccoli florets**,
   steamed
2 cups **sugar snap peas**,
   steamed

Preheat the slow cooker if necessary. Spray a large skillet with a little low-calorie cooking oil spray and place over high heat until hot. Add the beef, a few pieces at a time until all the beef is in the pan, and cook for 5 minutes, stirring, until browned. Use a slotted spoon to transfer the beef to the slow cooker pot.

Add a little more low-calorie cooking oil spray to the pan, add the onion and cook for 4–5 minutes, until beginning to brown. Add the rutabaga, carrots, and mushrooms and cook for 2 minutes. Add the flour and stir well.

Stir in the stock, vinegar, and mustard, season to taste and bring to a boil. Pour over the beef in the slow cooker pot. Arrange the potato slices on top, slightly overlapping. Season lightly, then press the potatoes into the stock.

Cover and cook on High for 7–8 hours, until the potatoes and beef are tender. Spray the potatoes with a little extra low-calorie cooking oil spray, then place the slow cooker pot under a preheated hot broiler until the potatoes are golden. Sprinkle with the parsley and serve with the steamed vegetables.

For mustard beef hotpot, follow the recipe above, using 1 tablespoon whole-grain mustard in place of the balsamic vinegar and dry mustard. **Calories per serving 409**

spiced beef & red pepper stew

Calories per serving **469**
Serves **4**
Preparation time **20 minutes**
Cooking time **8–10 hours**

low-calorie cooking oil spray
1 lb **stewing beef**, trimmed of
   fat and cubed
2 **red onions**, cut into wedges
2 **celery sticks**, thickly sliced
2 **red bell peppers**, cored,
   seeded, and cut into chunks
2 **garlic cloves**, finely chopped
1 teaspoon **cumin seeds**,
   coarsely crushed
1 teaspoon **chili powder**
2 teaspoons **all-purpose flour**
2 cups **beef stock**
1 tablespoon **tomato paste**
salt and **pepper**

To serve
¼ cup chopped **fresh cilantro**
1¼ cups **long-grain rice**,
   boiled

Preheat the slow cooker if necessary. Spray a large skillet with a little low-calorie cooking oil spray and place over high heat until hot. Add the beef, a few pieces at a time until all the beef is in the pan, and cook for 5 minutes, stirring, until browned. Use a slotted spoon to transfer the beef to the slow cooker pot.

Add a little more low-calorie cooking oil spray to the pan, add the onion wedges and cook for 2–3 minutes, stirring. Add the celery and bell pepper, then stir in the garlic, cumin, and chili powder and cook for 1 minute.

Stir in the flour, then add the stock and tomato paste, season to taste and bring to a boil, stirring. Spoon over the beef, cover, and cook on Low for 8–10 hours, until the beef is tender.

Stir the chopped cilantro into the cooked rice and spoon into shallow bowls. Stir the beef casserole, spoon over the rice and serve.

For Chinese gingered beef, follow the recipe above, replacing the cumin seeds and chili powder with 2 tablespoons soy sauce and 2 tablespoons finely chopped fresh ginger root. Serve with 8 oz Chinese egg noodles, cooked according to package instructions. **Calories per serving 490**

pulled pork

Calories per serving **408**
Serves **4**
Preparation time **15 minutes**
Cooking time **5–6 hours**

1 lb 6 oz boneless **pork shoulder joint**, trimmed of fat
1 tablespoon **molasses**
½ teaspoon **ground allspice**
½ teaspoon **ground ginger**
½ teaspoon **ground cumin**
½ teaspoon **dried red pepper flakes**
¼ teaspoon **salt**
leaves from 2–3 **thyme sprigs**
1 **onion**, sliced
¾ cup hot **chicken stock**
pepper

To serve
4 **hamburger buns**, split
4 **lettuce leaves**, shredded
3 **tomatoes**, thinly sliced
1 **dill cucumber**, drained and sliced

Preheat the slow cooker if necessary. Unroll the pork joint and make a cut through the middle to reduce the thickness by half. Place in the slow cooker pot and spread with the molasses.

Mix the ground spices, red pepper flakes, salt, and thyme leaves and season with pepper. Rub over the pork joint, then tuck the onion slices around it. Pour the hot stock over the onions, then cover and cook on High for 5–6 hours or until the pork is very tender.

Place the pork on a chopping board and pull into shreds using two forks. Top the bottom halves of the buns with the lettuce, tomato, and dill cucumber, then pile the hot pork on top. Add a few of the onion slices to each bun and drizzle with the cooking juices. Replace the tops of the buns and serve immediately.

For herby pulled pork, follow the recipe above to prepare the pork and spread it with the molasses. Mix the red pepper flakes, salt, and thyme leaves with 2 finely chopped sage sprigs and rub over the molasses-spread pork. Add the onion and stock and continue as above. **Calories per serving 408**

warming lamb pot roast

Calories per serving **417**
Serves **4**
Preparation time **20 minutes**
Cooking time **5–6 hours**

low-calorie cooking oil spray
1¾ lb **leg of lamb** on the bone
1 **leek**, thickly sliced
2 teaspoons **all-purpose flour**
2 cups **lamb stock**
1 tablespoon **red currant jelly**
2½ tablespoons **mint leaves**,
chopped, plus extra to
garnish
7 oz **celeriac**, cut into ¾ inch
cubes
7 oz **rutabaga**, cut into ¾ inch
cubes
10 oz **baby Chantenay
carrots**, halved lengthwise
salt and **pepper**

Preheat the slow cooker if necessary. Spray a large skillet with a little low-calorie cooking oil spray and place over high heat until hot. Season the lamb and seal in the hot pan for 5–10 minutes, turning until browned on all sides. Transfer to the slow cooker pot.

Add the white leek slices (reserving the green slices) to the skillet with a little extra low-calorie cooking oil spray, cook for 2–3 minutes, then sprinkle in the flour and stir well. Add the stock, red currant jelly, and mint, then bring to a boil, stirring.

Arrange the celeriac, rutabaga, and carrots around the lamb, then pour over the leeks and stock. Cover and cook on High for 5–6 hours, until the lamb starts to fall off the bone and the vegetables are tender, adding the reserved green leek slices for the last 15 minutes of cooking.

Serve the lamb in shallow bowls with the hot vegetables and stock, garnished with extra mint. If you prefer a thicker sauce, drain the stock into a small saucepan and boil rapidly to reduce by half.

For lamb pot roast with flageolet beans, follow the recipe above, adding 15 oz can of flageolet beans, drained, 2 rosemary sprigs and 2 finely chopped garlic cloves instead of the mint, rutabaga, and celeriac.
Calories per serving 459

skinny spaghetti bolognese

Calories per serving **490**
Serves **4**
Preparation time **20 minutes**
Cooking time **8–10 hours**

low-calorie cooking oil spray
1 lb **extra-lean ground beef**
1 **onion**, finely chopped
2 **garlic cloves**, finely chopped
1 **carrot**, finely grated
2 **zucchini**, finely grated
¾ cup sliced **button mushrooms**
2 cups **tomato puree or sauce**
⅔ cup **beef stock**
1 teaspoon **dried oregano**
salt and **pepper**

To serve
10 oz **dried spaghetti**
handful of **oregano** or **basil leaves**

Preheat the slow cooker if necessary. Spray a large skillet with a little low-calorie cooking oil spray and place over high heat until hot. Add the ground beef and onion and cook for 5 minutes, stirring and breaking up the meat with a wooden spoon until evenly browned.

Stir in the garlic, carrot, zucchini and mushrooms. Add the tomato puree or sauce, stock, and oregano, then season to taste. Bring to the boil, stirring. Transfer to the slow cooker pot, cover, and cook on Low for 8–10 hours.

Cook the spaghetti in a large saucepan of lightly salted boiling water according to package instructions, until tender. Drain well, toss with the Bolognese sauce, and serve immediately sprinkled with oregano or basil leaves.

For Italian shepherd's pie, make the Bolognese sauce as above. Peel 1 lb potatoes and 1 lb rutabaga and cut into chunks. Cook in a saucepan of lightly salted boiling water for 15–20 minutes, until tender. Drain and mash with ¼ cup vegetable stock (or ¼ cup cooking water). Beat 1 egg and stir half into the mash, then season to taste. Spoon the mash over the Bolognese sauce and rough up the top with a fork. Brush with the remaining beaten egg and brown under the broiler before serving. **Calories per serving 258**

french-style chicken pot roast

Calories per serving **495**
Serves **4**
Preparation time **20 minutes**
Cooking time **5¼–6¼ hours**

2 lb 10 oz **oven-ready chicken**

7½ oz **baby new potatoes**, halved

1 **red bell pepper**, cored, seeded, and diced

1 **yellow bell pepper**, cored, seeded, and diced

4 **garlic cloves**, halved

1 cup **cherry tomatoes**, halved

½ **lemon**, sliced

small bunch of **basil**

1¼ cups hot **chicken stock**

1 tablespoon **tomato paste**

1 tablespoons **granular sweetener**

¼ cup **pitted green olives** in brine, drained and halved

salt and **pepper**

Preheat the slow cooker if necessary. Put the chicken into the slow cooker pot, then tuck the potatoes, peppers, garlic, and tomatoes around it. Season the chicken with salt and pepper, then arrange the lemon slices over the breast. Tear half the basil into pieces and sprinkle over the chicken and vegetables.

Mix the hot stock with the tomato paste and sweetener, then pour into the slow cooker pot and add the olives. Cover and cook on High for 5–6 hours or until the chicken is thoroughly cooked and the meat juices run clear when the thickest parts of the leg and breast are pierced with a sharp knife.

Place the slow cooker pot under a preheated hot broiler until the chicken is golden. Cut the meat off the bones and arrange it in shallow bowls with the vegetables and stock, garnished with the remaining basil. If you prefer a thicker sauce, drain the stock into a small saucepan and boil rapidly to reduce by half.

For lemon & tarragon pot-roasted chicken, place the chicken in the slow cooker pot and tuck 7½ oz halved baby new potatoes, 3 chopped carrots, 3 chopped celery sticks, and 2 tarragon sprigs around it. Season the chicken and cover the breast with ½ sliced lemon. Mix 1¼ cups hot chicken stock with 1 tablespoon tomato paste and 1 tablespoon Dijon mustard and pour over the chicken. Cook as above and serve garnished with extra tarragon. **Calories per serving 470**

tipsy mustard pork

Calories per serving **423**
Serves **4**
Preparation time **20 minutes**
Cooking time **4–5 hours**

low-calorie cooking oil spray
4 **pork loin chops** on the
bone, 7½ oz each, trimmed
of fat
1 **onion**, chopped
1 tablespoon **all-purpose
flour**
2 teaspoons **whole-grain
mustard**
1 teaspoon **ground turmeric**
⅔ cup **hard cider**
1¼ cups **chicken stock**
1 lb **rutabaga**, cut into 1 inch
pieces
8 oz **potatoes**, cut into 1 inch
pieces
1 **dessert apple**, cored and
thickly sliced
salt and **pepper**
7 oz **sugar snap peas**,
steamed, to serve

Preheat the slow cooker if necessary. Spray a large skillet with a little low-calorie cooking oil spray and place over high heat until hot. Add the chops in a single layer, cook for 5 minutes, turning once, until browned on both sides, then transfer to a plate.

Add a little extra low-calorie cooking oil spray to the pan if necessary, then add the onion and cook over medium heat for 4–5 minutes, until softened. Stir in the flour, then add the mustard, turmeric, cider, and stock. Season to taste and bring to a boil, stirring.

Place the rutabaga and potato in the slow cooker pot. Arrange the pork chops in a single layer on top, then add the apple slices. Pour over the hot stock mixture, cover, and cook on High for 4–5 hours, until the pork is very tender.

Transfer the pork to a plate. Divide the vegetables among 4 shallow dishes, top with the chops and drizzle with the sauce. Serve with steamed sugar snap peas.

For mustard chicken with celeriac, follow the recipe above, browning 4 skinless chicken leg joints in the skillet instead of the pork chops. Continue, replacing the rutabaga with 1 lb diced celeriac. Cook on Low for 8–10 hours, until the chicken is cooked through with no hint of pink juices and the celeriac is tender. **Calories per serving 413**

pork puttanesca

Calories per serving **403**
Serves **4**
Preparation time **20 minutes**
Cooking time **7–8 hours**

low-calorie cooking oil spray
1¼ lb **lean pork**, diced
1 **onion**, chopped
2 **garlic cloves**, finely chopped
14½ oz can **diced tomatoes**
4 teaspoons **sherry vinegar**
½ cup **basil**, coarsely torn,
    plus extra to garnish
1 tablespoon **capers** in brine,
    drained and chopped
⅓ cup **pitted olives**, chopped
salt and **pepper**
chopped **parsley**, to garnish
6 oz **spaghetti**, boiled

Preheat the slow cooker if necessary. Spray a large skillet with a little low-calorie cooking oil spray and place over high heat until hot. Add the pork, a few pieces at a time until all the pork is in the pan, and cook for 5 minutes, stirring, until browned. Use a slotted spoon to transfer the pork to a plate.

Add a little more low-calorie cooking oil spray to the skillet if necessary, then add the onion and cook for 4–5 minutes, stirring, until just beginning to brown. Add the garlic, tomatoes, vinegar, and basil and bring to a boil, stirring.

Mix the capers and olives together and add half to the sauce, reserving the rest for garnish.

Transfer the pork to the slow cooker pot, then pour over the sauce. Cover and cook on High for 7–8 hours, until the pork is tender. Stir, then sprinkle with the reserved capers and olives, some extra basil, and a little chopped parsley. Serve with the cooked spaghetti.

For pork osso bucco, follow the recipe above, using 2 tablespoons chopped parsley mixed with the grated zest of 1 lemon and 2 finely chopped garlic cloves instead of the capers and olives. Serve with 1 cup rice, boiled with a few strands of saffron. **Calories per serving 436**

lamb steaks with cumberland sauce

Calories per serving **441**
Serves **4**
Preparation time **20 minutes**
Cooking time **8¼–10¼ hours**

1 tablespoon **sunflower oil**
1 lb 9 oz **lamb rump steaks**,
   trimmed of fat
1 **onion**, sliced
2 teaspoons **all-purpose flour**
½ cup **red wine**
½ cup **lamb stock**
finely shredded zest and juice
   of 1 **orange**
finely shredded zest and juice
   of 1 **lemon**
1 inch piece of **fresh ginger
   root**, finely chopped
1 tablespoon **tomato paste**
1 tablespoon **red currant jelly**
1 tablespoon **granular
   sweetener**
salt and **pepper**
1½ lb **celeriac**, diced, to serve

Preheat the slow cooker if necessary. Heat the oil in a large skillet over high heat until hot. Add the lamb and cook for 2–3 minutes, turning once, until browned on both sides. Use a slotted spoon to transfer the lamb to the slow cooker pot.

Add the onion to the pan and cook for 4–5 minutes over medium heat, stirring until softened. Stir in the flour, then add the wine, stock, half the orange and lemon zest, the orange and lemon juice, the ginger, tomato paste, red currant jelly, and sweetener. Season to taste with salt and pepper and bring to the boil, stirring. Pour the mixture over the lamb, cover, and cook on Low for 8–10 hours.

Cook the celeriac in a saucepan of lightly salted boiling water for 10–15 minutes until tender. Mash with a little of the cooking water until smooth and season to taste. Serve with the lamb in bowls, garnished with the remaining orange and lemon zest.

For lamb steaks with cranberry sauce, follow the recipe above, using 3 tablespoons dried cranberries and 1 tablespoon cranberry sauce instead of the ginger and red currant jelly. Cook and serve as above. **Calories per serving 444**

peasant paella

Calories per serving **499**
Serves **4**
Preparation time **20 minutes**
Cooking time **5–6¼ hours**

low-calorie cooking oil spray
1 lb boneless, skinless
 chicken thighs, cubed
1 **onion**, chopped
2¼ oz **chorizo**, sliced
2 **garlic cloves**, finely chopped
1 **red bell pepper**, cored,
 seeded, and diced
1 **orange bell pepper**, cored,
 seeded, and diced
2 **celery sticks**, diced
2 pinches of **saffron threads**
½ teaspoon **dried**
 Mediterranean herbs
3 cups hot **chicken stock**
scant 1 cup **long-grain brown**
 rice
1 cup **frozen peas**
salt and **pepper**
2 tablespoons **chopped**
 parsley, to garnish

Preheat the slow cooker if necessary. Spray a large skillet with a little low-calorie cooking oil spray and place over high heat until hot. Add the chicken, a few pieces at a time until all the chicken is in the pan, and cook for 5 minutes, stirring, until browned. Use a slotted spoon to transfer the chicken to the slow cooker pot.

Add the onion, chorizo, and garlic to the skillet and cook for 3–4 minutes, stirring until the onion is beginning to color. Add the peppers and celery, stir well, then transfer to the slow cooker pot. Mix the saffron and dried herbs with the hot stock, season to taste, then pour into the slow cooker pot and stir well. Cover and cook on High for 3–4 hours.

Place the rice in a sieve and rinse under cold running water, then stir into the chicken mixture. Cover again and cook for 1½–1¾ hours, until the rice is tender. Stir in the peas and continue cooking for 15 minutes. Serve garnished with chopped parsley.

For seafood paella, follow the recipe above to cook the paella, omitting the chicken. Defrost 13 oz frozen mixed seafood and pat dry on paper towels. Spray a large skillet with a little low-calorie cooking oil spray and place over high heat until hot. Add the seafood and cook for 4–5 minutes until piping hot. Stir into the finished paella and garnish with the parsley.
Calories per serving 385

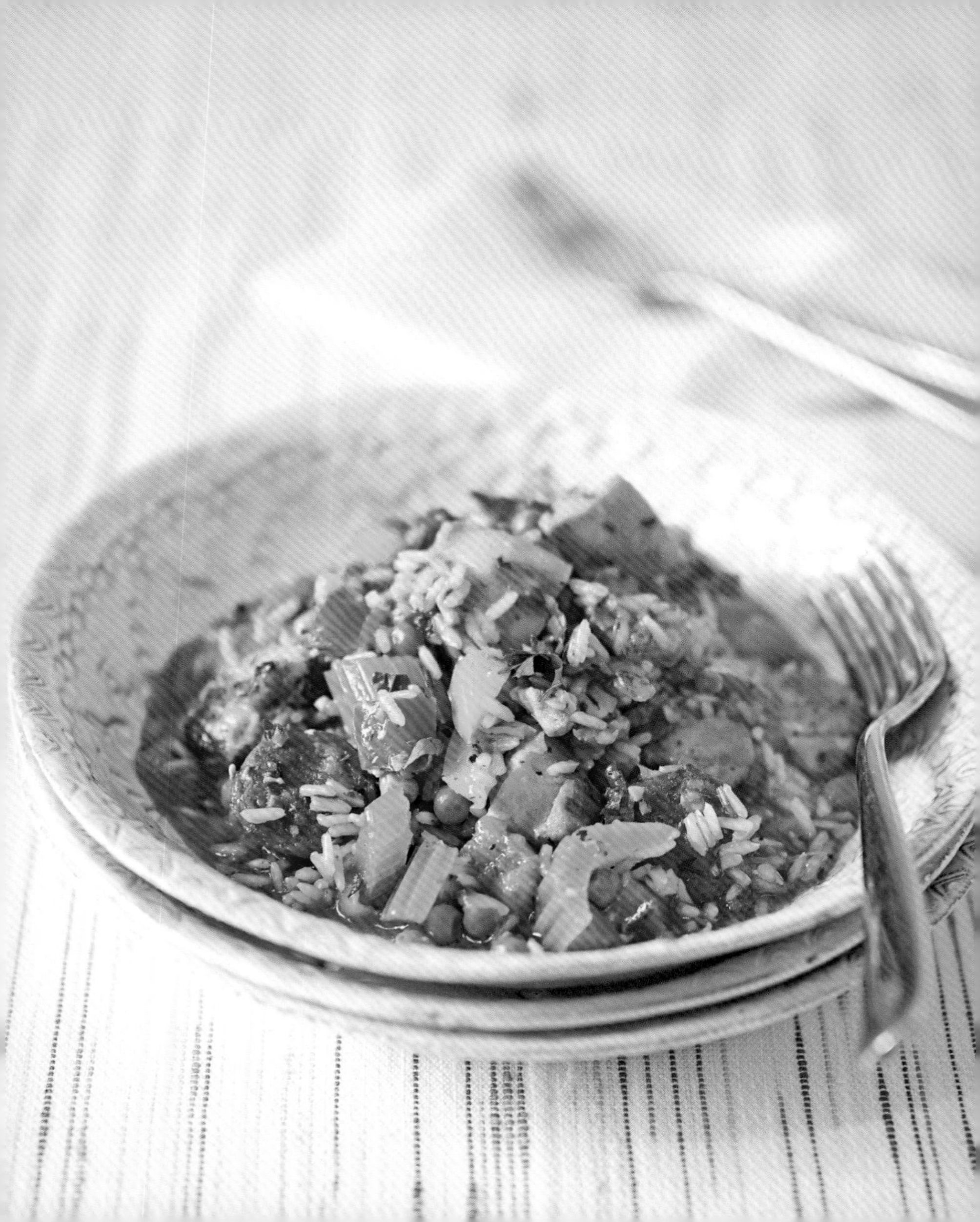

chicken cacciatore

Calories per serving **453**
Serves **4**
Preparation time **20 minutes**
Cooking time **8–9 hours**

low-calorie cooking oil spray
1 lb boneless, skinless
  chicken thighs, cubed
1 **onion**, chopped
2 **garlic cloves**, finely chopped
1 **red bell pepper**, cored,
  seeded, and diced
1 **orange bell pepper**, cored,
  seeded, and diced
2 **celery sticks**, diced
2/3 cup **chicken stock**
14½ oz can **diced tomatoes**
1 tablespoon **tomato paste**
1 tablespoon **balsamic
  vinegar**
leaves from 2 **rosemary
  sprigs**, chopped
salt and **pepper**
2 tablespoons chopped
  parsley, to garnish
7 oz **dried tagliatelle**, to serve

Preheat the slow cooker if necessary. Spray a large skillet with a little low-calorie cooking oil spray and place over high heat until hot. Add the chicken, a few pieces at a time until all the chicken is in the pan, and cook for 3–4 minutes, stirring, until just beginning to brown. Add the onion and continue to cook until the chicken is golden and the onion has softened.

Stir in the garlic, peppers, and celery, then add the stock, tomatoes, tomato paste, balsamic vinegar, and rosemary. Season generously and bring to a boil, stirring. Transfer to the slow cooker pot, cover, and cook on Low for 8–9 hours, until the chicken is tender and cooked through.

Meanwhile, cook the tagliatelle in a saucepan of lightly salted boiling water according to package instructions until tender. Drain, then toss with the chicken mixture and serve garnished with parsley.

For potato-topped cacciatore, follow the recipe above and place all the ingredients in the slow cooker pot. Thinly slice 1¼ lb potatoes and arrange them on top of the chicken mixture, overlapping. Press the potatoes down into the liquid, then cover and cook on High for 5–6 hours, until the potatoes and chicken are cooked through. Spray the potatoes with a little extra low-calorie cooking oil spray, then place the slow cooker pot under a hot broiler until the potatoes are golden, if desired.
Calories per serving 403

spicy turkey tortillas

Calories per serving **468**
Serves **4**
Preparation time **20 minutes**
Cooking time **8¼–10¼ hours**

low-calorie cooking oil spray
13 oz **ground turkey breast**
1 **onion**, chopped
2 **garlic cloves**, finely chopped
1 teaspoon **dried red pepper flakes**
1 teaspoon **cumin seeds**, crushed
1 teaspoon **mild paprika**
14½ oz can **diced tomatoes**
8 oz can **red kidney beans**, drained
⅔ cup **chicken stock**
1 tablespoon **tomato paste**
1 **red bell pepper**, cored, seeded, and diced

To serve
4 x 8 inch **soft tortilla wraps**, 1½ oz each
2 cups **salad greens**
¼ cup **0% fat Greek yogurt**
⅓ cup shredded **reduced-fat cheddar cheese**
fresh cilantro, torn

Preheat the slow cooker if necessary. Spray a large skillet with a little low-calorie cooking oil spray and place over high heat until hot. Add the ground turkey and onion and fry for 4–5 minutes, stirring and breaking up the meat with a wooden spoon until it is just beginning to brown.

Stir in the garlic, pepper flakes, cumin seeds and paprika, then add the tomatoes, kidney beans, stock, and tomato paste. Add the red bell pepper, season to taste with salt and pepper, and bring to a boil. Transfer to the slow cooker pot, cover, and cook on Low for 8–10 hours until the turkey is cooked through.

Warm the tortillas in a hot dry skillet for 1–2 minutes each side, then place on 4 serving plates. Spoon the spicy turkey on top, then add a handful of salad greens to each, a spoonful of yogurt, a little cheddar, and some torn cilantro. Serve immediately.

For spicy turkey thatch, follow the recipe above to make and cook the spicy turkey mixture. Cook, drain, and mash 1½ lb potatoes, stir in ¼ cup vegetable stock and season to taste. Place the turkey mixture in a shallow heatproof dish and spoon the mashed potato on top. Rough up the top with a fork, then brush with ½ beaten egg. Brown under the broiler before serving.
Calories per serving 440

sticky jerk ribs

Calories per serving **435**
Serves **4**
Preparation time **20 minutes**
Cooking time **5¼–6¼ hours**

2½ lb **lean pork ribs**
1 **onion**, cut into wedges
1 large **carrot**, sliced
3 **bay leaves**
2 tablespoons **malt vinegar**
low-calorie cooking oil spray
salt and **pepper**

Jerk glaze
½ cup **tomato puree or sauce**
3 tablespoons **soy sauce**
½ teaspoon **ground cinnamon**
½ teaspoon **ground allspice**
¼ teaspoon **chili powder**
1 tablespoon packed **dark brown sugar**
grated zest and juice of ½ **orange**
4 **scallions**, finely chopped

Preheat the slow cooker if necessary. Place the pork ribs, onion, and carrot in the slow cooker pot and add the bay leaves and vinegar. Season generously, then pour over enough boiling water to cover the ribs, making sure the level is at least 1 inch from the top of the pot. Cover and cook on High for 5–6 hours until the meat is starting to fall away from the bones. Transfer the ribs to a foil-lined broiler pan or baking sheet.

Mix together the glaze ingredients, then brush all over the ribs. Spray with a little low-calorie cooking oil spray and cook under a preheated hot broiler, with the ribs about 2 inches away from the heat, for about 10 minutes, turning from time to time and brushing with the pan juices until a deep brown. Serve with salad, if desired.

For sticky hoisin ribs, follow the recipe above to cook the ribs in the slow cooker. Make a glaze by mixing together 3 tablespoons hoisin sauce, 8 tablespoons tomato puree or sauce, ¼ teaspoon chili powder, grated zest and juice of ½ orange and 4 finely chopped scallions. Brush over the ribs and broiler as above.
Calories per serving 436

turkey kheema mutter

Calories per serving **454**
Serves **4**
Preparation time **15 minutes**
Cooking time **8½–10½ hours**

low-calorie cooking oil spray
1 lb **ground turkey breast**
1 **onion**, chopped
2 **garlic cloves**, finely chopped
1 inch piece of **fresh ginger root**, finely chopped
1 teaspoon **cumin seeds**, crushed
4 teaspoons **medium-hot curry powder**
2 cups **tomato puree or sauce**
2 teaspoons **granular sweetener**
1 cup **frozen peas**
¼ cup chopped **fresh cilantro**
salt and **pepper**
½ **red onion**, thinly sliced, to garnish
4 small **chapatis**, 2 oz each, to serve

Preheat the slow cooker if necessary. Spray a large skillet with a little low-calorie cooking oil spray and place over high heat until hot. Add the ground turkey and onion and fry for 4–5 minutes, stirring and breaking up the meat with a wooden spoon until it is just beginning to brown.

Stir in the garlic, ginger, cumin, and curry powder and cook for 1 minute, then add the tomato puree or sauce and sweetener. Season to taste and bring to a boil, stirring. Transfer to the slow cooker pot, cover and cook on Low for 8–10 hours, until the turkey is cooked through.

Add the frozen peas to the slow cooker pot with half the cilantro. Cover again and cook on High for 15 minutes. Sprinkle with the remaining cilantro and the red onion and serve with the chapatis.

For kheema mutter jackets, follow the recipe above to make and cook the turkey and pea mixture. Scrub and prick 4 baking potatoes, 6 oz each, place in the microwave on a sheet of paper towel and cook on full power for about 20 minutes, until tender. Transfer to serving plates, cut in half and top with the kheema mutter, remaining cilantro and sliced red onion. **Calories per serving 399**

sweet & sour chicken

Calories per serving **459**
Serves **4**
Preparation time **20 minutes**
Cooking time **6½–8½ hours**

1 tablespoon **sunflower oil**
2 lb boneless, skinless
   chicken thighs, cubed
4 **scallions**, thickly sliced
2 **carrots**, halved lengthwise
   and thinly sliced
1 inch piece of **fresh ginger
   root**, finely chopped
14 oz can **pineapple chunks**
   in natural juice
1¼ cups **chicken stock**
1 tablespoon **cornstarch**
1 tablespoon **tomato paste**
2 tablespoons **sugar**
2 tablespoons **soy sauce**
2 tablespoons **malt vinegar**
1¾ cups canned **bamboo
   shoots**, drained
1 cup **bean sprouts**
1 cup **snow peas**, thinly sliced
¾ cup **rice**, boiled

Preheat the slow cooker if necessary. Heat the oil in a large skillet over high heat, add the chicken and cook for 3–4 minutes, until browned on all sides. Add the white scallion slices (reserving the green slices), the carrots, and ginger and cook for 2 minutes.

Stir in the pineapple chunks and their juice and the stock. Put the cornstarch, tomato paste, and sugar in a small bowl, then mix in the soy sauce and vinegar to make a smooth paste. Add to the pan and bring to a boil, stirring.

Transfer the chicken mixture to the slow cooker pot, add the bamboo shoots and press the chicken pieces into the liquid. Cover and cook on Low for 6–8 hours, until the chicken is cooked through.

Add the reserved green scallion slices, the bean sprouts, and snow peas and mix well. Cover again and cook for 15 minutes or until the vegetables are just tender. Serve with the boiled rice.

For lemon chicken, follow the recipe above as far as the addition of the chicken stock. Mix the cornstarch to a smooth paste with the juice of 1 lemon, then stir into the pan with 2 tablespoons dry sherry and 4 teaspoons sugar. Bring to the boil, stirring, then transfer to the slow cooker pot and cook as above, adding the green scallion slices, bean sprouts and snow peas at the end.
Calories per serving 438

beery barley beef

Calories per serving **439**
Serves **4**
Preparation time **15 minutes**
Cooking time **9–10 hours**

1 tablespoon **sunflower oil**
1¼ lb **lean stewing beef,**
  cubed
1 **onion**, chopped
1 tablespoon **all-purpose**
  flour
1⅔ cups **carrots**, diced
1⅔ cups **parsnips** or
  potatoes, diced
1¼ cups **light ale**
3 cups **beef stock**
small bunch of **mixed herbs**
  or **dried bouquet garni**
½ cup **pearl barley**
salt and **pepper**

Preheat the slow cooker if necessary. Heat the oil in a skillet, add the beef a few pieces at a time until it is all in the pan, then fry over high heat, stirring, until browned. Remove the beef with a slotted spoon and transfer to the slow cooker pot.

Add the onion to the skillet and fry, stirring, for 5 minutes or until lightly browned. Mix in the flour, then add the root vegetables and beer and bring to a boil, stirring. Pour into the slow cooker pot.

Add the stock to the skillet with the herbs and a little salt and pepper, bring to a boil, then pour into the slow cooker pot. Add the pearl barley, cover with the lid, and cook on low for 9–10 hours, until the beef is tender. Serve with herb croutons, if desired.

For herb croutons to accompany the beef, beat 2 tablespoons chopped parsley, 2 tablespoons chopped chives, and 1 tablespoon chopped tarragon and a little black pepper into 5 tablespoons soft butter. Thickly slice ½ French loaf, toast lightly on both sides, then spread with the herb butter. **Calories per serving 433**

tuna arrabiata

Calories per serving **481**
Serves **4**
Preparation time **20 minutes**
Cooking time **4–5 hours**

1 tablespoon **olive oil**
1 **onion**, chopped
2 **garlic cloves**, finely chopped
1 **red bell pepper**, cored,
  seeded, and diced
1 teaspoon **smoked paprika**
1/4–1/2 teaspoon **dried red**
  pepper flakes
14 1/2 oz can **diced tomatoes**
2/3 cup **vegetable** or **fish**
  stock
7 oz can **tuna** in water, drained
salt and **pepper**

To serve
12 oz **dried spaghetti**
1/4 cup grated **Parmesan**
  cheese
small handful of **basil leaves**

Preheat the slow cooker if necessary. Heat the oil in a large skillet over medium heat, add the onion and cook, stirring, for 5 minutes or until just browning around the edges. Add the garlic, bell pepper, paprika, and dried pepper and cook for 2 minutes.

Add the tomatoes and stock and season to taste. Bring to a boil, then transfer to the slow cooker pot. Break the tuna into large pieces and stir into the tomato mixture. Cover and cook on Low for 4–5 hours.

Meanwhile, cook the spaghetti in a saucepan of lightly salted boiling water according to package instructions until tender. Drain and stir into the tomato sauce. Spoon into shallow bowls and sprinkle with the grated Parmesan and basil leaves.

For double tomato arrabiata, follow the recipe above using 1 1/2 cups sliced sun-dried tomatoes and 1 1/2 cups sliced button mushrooms instead of the tuna. Cook and serve as above. **Calories per serving 479**

smoked mackerel kedgeree

Calories per serving **492**
Serves **4**
Preparation time **15 minutes**
Cooking time **3½–4½ hours**

1 tablespoon **sunflower oil**
1 **onion**, chopped
1 teaspoon **ground turmeric**
2 tablespoons **mango chutney**
about 3 cups **vegetable stock**
1 **bay leaf**
¾ cup **easy-cook brown rice**
7 oz **smoked mackerel fillets**, skinned
⅔ cup **frozen peas**
½ cup **watercress** or **arugula leaves**
4 **hard-cooked eggs**, cut into wedges
salt and **pepper**

Preheat the slow cooker if necessary. Heat the oil in a large skillet over a medium heat, add the onion and cook, stirring, for 5 minutes, until softened. Add the turmeric, chutney, stock, and bay leaf, season to taste with salt and pepper, and bring to a boil.

Pour into the slow cooker pot and add the rice. Arrange the smoked mackerel in the pot in a single layer, cover and cook on Low for 3–4 hours, until the rice is tender and has absorbed almost all the stock.

Stir in the peas, breaking up the fish into chunky pieces. Add a little extra hot stock if the rice is very dry, cover again and cook for 15 minutes. Stir in the watercress or arugula, spoon onto plates, and top with the egg wedges.

For smoked haddock kedgeree with cardamom, follow the recipe above, increasing the amount of rice to a scant cup and using 4 crushed cardamom pods with their black seeds instead of the chutney. Replace the smoked mackerel with 13 oz skinned smoked haddock fillet, cut into 2 pieces. Continue as above, omitting the arugula or watercress. Drizzle with ¼ cup cream before serving. **Calories per serving 418**

new orleans chicken gumbo

Calories per serving **414 (not including rice)**
Serves **4**
Preparation time **20 minutes**
Cooking time **8½–10½ hours**

2 tablespoons **olive oil**
1 lb boneless, skinless **chicken thighs**, cubed
3 oz **chorizo**, diced
3 oz **smoked bacon**, trimmed of fat and diced
1 **onion**, sliced
2 **garlic cloves**, chopped
2 tablespoons **all-purpose flour**
2½ cups **chicken stock**
2 **bay leaves**
2 **thyme sprigs**
¼–½ teaspoon **cayenne pepper**
3 **celery sticks**, sliced
½ each of 3 different colored **bell peppers**, cored, seeded, and sliced
1 cup thickly sliced **okra**, (optional)
salt
chopped **parsley**, to garnish

Preheat the slow cooker if necessary. Heat the oil in a large skillet over high heat, add the chicken a few pieces at time until all the chicken is in the pan, then add the chorizo and bacon and cook for 5 minutes, stirring, until the chicken is golden. Transfer to the slow cooker pot with a slotted spoon.

Add the onion to the skillet and cook over medium heat until softened. Mix in the garlic, then stir in the flour. Gradually add the stock, stirring, then add the herbs and cayenne, to taste, and season generously with salt and pepper. Bring to a boil, stirring.

Add the celery and peppers to the slow cooker pot, then pour over the hot onion mixture. Cover and cook on Low for 8–10 hours or until the chicken is cooked through.

Stir in the okra, if using, cover again and cook on High for 15 minutes or until the okra has just softened. Stir once more, then sprinkle with chopped parsley. Serve with rice, if desired.

For shrimp gumbo soup, follow the recipe above omitting the chicken and replacing the chicken stock with 2½ cups fish stock, and adding 2 sliced carrots, 2 diced sweet potatoes, and 1 diced zucchini to the slow cooker pot with the celery and peppers. Add 7 oz large cooked peeled shrimp to the pot with the okra, if using, and cook on High for 20–30 minutes or until the shrimp are piping hot. Serve with rice, if desired.
Calories per serving 433

turkey tagine

Calories per serving **401**
  (not including couscous)
Serves **4**
Preparation time **25 minutes**
Cooking time **6¼–7¼ hours**

1 **turkey drumstick**, 1 lb 6 oz
1 tablespoon **olive oil**
1 **onion**, chopped
2 **garlic cloves**, finely chopped
1 inch piece of **fresh ginger
  root**, finely chopped
2 tablespoons **all-purpose
  flour**
1 teaspoon **ground turmeric**
1 teaspoon **ground cinnamon**
1 teaspoon **ground cilantro**
½ teaspoon **cumin seeds**
2½ cups hot **chicken stock**
15 oz can **chickpeas**, drained
1⅓ cups **parsnips**, diced
1⅓ cups **carrots**, diced
small bunch of **fresh cilantro**,
  coarsely chopped
salt and **pepper**

Check that the turkey drumstick will fit into the slow cooker pot before you begin, cutting off the knuckle end if necessary with a large knife, after hitting it with a rolling pin or hammer. Preheat the slow cooker if necessary.

Heat the oil in a skillet over high heat, add the drumstick and cook, turning, until golden-brown all over. Transfer to the slow cooker pot. Add the onion to the pan and cook over medium heat for 5 minutes until softened. Stir in the garlic, ginger, and flour, then mix in the spices. Gradually stir in the stock, season to taste, and bring to a boil.

Pour the onion mixture over the turkey. Add the chickpeas and vegetables to the pot and press into the liquid. Cover and cook on High for 6–7 hours or until the meat is tender and almost falling off the bone.

Take the turkey meat off the bone, discarding the skin and tendons. Cut it into bite-size pieces and return them to the slow cooker pot. Stir in the chopped cilantro and serve with couscous, if desired.

For chilied chicken tagine, follow the recipe above, using 4 skinless chicken thigh and drumstick joints instead of the turkey and adding ½ teaspoon smoked hot paprika with the other spices. Cook on High for 5–6 hours. **Calories per serving 401**

pot-roasted chicken with lemon

Calories per serving **481**
Serves **4**
Preparation time **25 minutes**
Cooking time **5–6 hours**

2 tablespoons **olive oil**
3 lb **oven-ready chicken**
1 large **onion**, cut into
  6 wedges
2 cups **hard cider**
1 tablespoon **Dijon mustard**
2 teaspoons **sugar**
3¾ cups hot **chicken stock**
3 **carrots**, cut into chunks
3 **celery sticks**, thickly sliced
1 **lemon**, cut into 6 wedges
6 **tarragon sprigs**
3 tablespoons **crème fraîche**
  or **sour cream**
salt and **pepper**

Preheat the slow cooker if necessary. Heat the oil in a large skillet over high heat, add the chicken and cook for 10 minutes, turning occasionally, until browned all over. Transfer to the slow cooker pot, breast side down.

Add the onion wedges to the pan and cook over medium heat for 3–4 minutes until lightly browned. Add the cider, mustard, and sugar and season to taste. Bring to a boil, stirring, then pour over the chicken.

Add the hot stock, then the vegetables, lemon wedges, and 3 sprigs of the tarragon, pressing the chicken and vegetables down into the liquid. Cover and cook on High for 5–6 hours or until the chicken is thoroughly cooked and the meat juices run clear when the thickest parts of the leg and breast are pierced with a sharp knife.

Transfer the chicken to a large serving plate and arrange the vegetables around it. Transfer 2½ cups of the hot cooking stock to a pitcher. Reserve a sprig of tarragon to garnish, then chop the remainder and whisk into the pitcher with the crème fraîche to make a gravy. Adjust the seasoning to taste. Serve the chicken and vegetables garnished with the remaining tarragon.

For herby pot-roasted chicken, follow the recipe above, omitting the lemon and tarragon, and adding a small bunch mixed herb sprigs, such as rosemary, sage or tarragon, and parsley or chives, to the slow cooker pot with the vegetables. Remove the herb sprigs before serving, and garnish the chicken with 3 tablespoons chopped parsley or chives. **Calories per serving 480**

fragrant spiced chicken

Calories per serving **490**
Serves **4**
Preparation time **15 minutes**
Cooking time **5¼–6¼ hours**

3 lb **oven-ready chicken**
1 **onion**, chopped
1⅓ cup **carrots**, sliced
3 inch piece of **fresh ginger root**, sliced
2 **garlic cloves**, sliced
1 large **mild red chile**, halved
3 large **star anise**
¼ cup **soy sauce**
¼ cup **rice vinegar**
1 tablespoon packed **light brown sugar**
3¾ cups boiling **water**
small bunch of **fresh cilantro**
1 cup **snow peas**, thickly sliced
2½ cups **bok choy**, thickly sliced
salt and **pepper**
7 oz **dried egg noodles**, to serve

Preheat the slow cooker if necessary. Place the chicken, breast side down, in the slow cooker pot. Add the onion, carrots, ginger, garlic, chile and star anise and spoon over the soy sauce, vinegar, and sugar. Pour over the boiling water.

Add the cilantro stems, reserving the leaves, and season to taste. Cover and cook on High for 5–6 hours or until the chicken is thoroughly cooked and the meat juices run clear when the thickest parts of the leg and breast are pierced with a sharp knife.

Transfer the chicken to a chopping board and keep warm. Add the snow peas and bok choy to the pot, cover again and cook for 5–10 minutes or until just wilted. Meanwhile, cook the noodles in a saucepan of lightly salted boiling water according to package instructions, drain well and divide among 4 bowls.

Carve the chicken into bite-size pieces and arrange on top of the noodles with the reserved cilantro leaves, then ladle over the hot broth and serve immediately.

For Italian spiced chicken with pesto, put the chicken into the pot with 1 chopped onion, 1⅓ cup sliced carrots, 2 sliced garlic cloves, 1 sliced fennel bulb, and 1 sliced lemon. Pour over the boiling water as above and replace the cilantro with a small bunch of basil. Use 3 chopped tomatoes, 1 cup chopped purple sprouting broccoli, and 2 tablespoons pesto sauce instead of the snow peas and bok choy. Cook 8 oz fresh tagliatelle according to package instructions to serve with the chicken. **Calories per serving 454**

sweet potato & egg curry

Calories per serving **451**
  (not including rice)
Serves **4**
Preparation time **15 minutes**
Cooking time **6½–8½ hours**

1 tablespoon **sunflower oil**
1 **onion**, chopped
1 teaspoon **cumin seeds**,
  coarsely crushed
1 teaspoon **ground cilantro**
1 teaspoon **ground turmeric**
1 teaspoon **garam masala**
½ teaspoon **dried red pepper**
  flakes
2 cups diced **sweet potatoes**
2 **garlic cloves**, finely chopped
14½ oz can **diced tomatoes**
14½ oz can **lentils**, drained
1¼ cups **vegetable stock**
1 teaspoon **sugar**
6 **hard-cooked eggs**, halved
1 cup **frozen peas**
⅔ cup **light cream**
small bunch of **fresh cilantro**,
  torn
salt and **pepper**

Preheat the slow cooker if necessary. Heat the oil in a skillet over medium heat, add the onion and cook for 5 minutes, until softened. Stir in the spices, sweet potatoes, and garlic and cook for 2 minutes, stirring.

Add the tomatoes, lentils, stock, and sugar and season to taste. Bring to a boil, stirring, then transfer to the slow cooker pot, cover, and cook on Low for 6–8 hours until the sweet potatoes are tender.

Add the eggs to the slow cooker pot with the peas, cream, and half the cilantro. Cover again and cook for 15 minutes more. Serve in bowls, garnished with the remaining cilantro.

For mixed vegetable curry, follow the recipe above, using 1 cup halved fine beans and ½ cup green shredded kale instead of the eggs, adding them to the slow cooker pot at the same time as the peas. **Calories per serving 335**

spiced date & chickpea pilaf

Calories per serving **442**
Serves **4**
Preparation time **15 minutes**
Cooking time **3–4 hours**

1 tablespoon **olive oil**
1 **onion**, chopped
1–2 **garlic cloves**, finely
chopped
1½ inch piece of **fresh ginger
root**, finely chopped
1 teaspoon **ground turmeric**
1 teaspoon **ground cumin**,
plus extra to garnish
1 teaspoon **ground cilantro**
1 cup **easy-cook brown rice**,
boiled
15 oz can **chickpeas**, drained
½ cup **pitted dates**, chopped
4 cups **vegetable stock**
salt and **pepper**

To serve
1 tablespoon **olive oil**
1 **onion**, thinly sliced
⅔ cup **0% fat Greek yogurt**
small handful of chopped
fresh cilantro

Preheat the slow cooker if necessary. Heat the oil in a large skillet over medium heat, add the onion and cook for 5 minutes, until softened. Stir in the garlic, ginger, and ground spices and cook for 1 minute.

Add the rice, chickpeas, dates, and stock, season to taste and bring to a boil, stirring. Pour into the slow cooker pot, cover, and cook on Low for 3–4 hours until the rice is tender and nearly all the stock has been absorbed.

Meanwhile, heat the remaining oil in a skillet over medium heat, add the sliced onion and cook, stirring, until crisp and golden.

Stir the pilaf, spoon into bowls and top each portion with a spoonful of yogurt, a little extra cumin, some crispy onions, and a little chopped cilantro.

For chicken & almond pilaf, follow the recipe above, adding 14½ oz diced boneless, skinless chicken thighs to the skillet with the chopped onion. Continue as above, omitting the dates. To serve, top with ¼ cup toasted sliced almonds and a little chopped mint instead of the crispy onions and cilantro. **Calories per serving 489**

tarka dahl

Calories per serving **490**
Serves **4**
Preparation time **15 minutes**
Cooking time **3–4 hours**

1 ¼ cups **dried red lentils**
1 **onion**, finely chopped
½ teaspoon **ground turmeric**
½ teaspoon **cumin seeds**,
   coarsely crushed
¾ inch piece of **fresh ginger
   root**, finely chopped
7 oz can **diced tomatoes**
2 ½ cups hot **vegetable stock**
salt and **pepper**
fresh cilantro leaves, torn,
   to garnish

Tarka

1 tablespoon **sunflower oil**
2 teaspoons **black mustard
   seeds**
½ teaspoon **cumin seeds**,
   coarsely crushed
pinch of **ground turmeric**
2 **garlic cloves**, finely chopped

To serve
⅔ cup **plain yogurt**
2 warm **naan breads**, halved

Preheat the slow cooker if necessary. Place the lentils in a sieve, rinse under cold running water, drain, then place in the slow cooker pot with the onion, spices, ginger, tomatoes, and hot stock. Season lightly, cover, and cook on High for 3–4 hours or until the lentils are soft and tender.

Meanwhile, heat the oil for the tarka in a small skillet, add the remaining tarka ingredients, and cook, stirring, for 2 minutes.

Coarsely mash the lentil mixture, then spoon into bowls. Top with spoonfuls of yogurt and drizzle with the tarka. Sprinkle with the cilantro leaves and serve with warm naan bread, if desired. (Calories per serving without naan 285.)

For tarka dahl with spinach, follow the recipe above to cook the lentils, adding 2 ½ cups washed and coarsely shredded spinach leaves for the last 15 minutes of cooking. Fry the tarka spices as above, adding ¼ teaspoon crushed dried red pepper flakes, if desired. **Calories per serving 295 (not including naan)**

oat & mixed seed granola

Calories per serving **459**
Serves **4**
Preparation time **15 minutes**
Cooking time **2½–3 hours**

¾ cup **medium oats**
½ cup **jumbo rolled oats**
¼ cup **pumpkin seeds**
3 tablespoons **sunflower seeds**
1½ tablespoons **golden flax seeds**
¼ teaspoon **ground cinnamon**
1 tablespoon **olive oil**
3 tablespoons **date syrup**
juice of ½ **orange**
¼ cup **dried goji berries**

To serve
2½ cups **skim milk**
sliced **banana**
sliced **strawberries**
raspberries

Preheat the slow cooker if necessary. Place the oats and seeds in the slow cooker pot and stir well. Add the cinnamon, olive oil, date syrup, and orange juice and mix again until thoroughly combined. Cover and cook on High for 1½–2 hours, stirring once or twice with a fork to break the mixture into clumps.

Remove the lid and cook for 1 hour more, until the granola is crisp. Break up once more with a fork, add the goji berries, then let cool. Store in an airtight jar in the refrigerator until ready to serve.

Serve in bowls, topped with skim milk and the fruit.

For honeyed oat & fruit granola, follow the recipe above, omitting the pumpkin seeds and using 3 tablespoons honey instead of the date syrup. Add 3 tablespoons dried cranberries and 1½ tablespoons dried cherries instead of the goji berries and serve as above. **Calories per serving 431**

pineapple upside-down puddings

Calories per serving **410**

Serves **4**

Preparation time **20 minutes**

Cooking time **2–2½ hours**

¼ cup **light corn syrup**

2 tablespoons packed **light brown sugar**

7½ oz can **pineapple chunks**, drained

3 tablespoons **candied cherries**, coarsely chopped

4 tablespoons **sunflower margarine**, plus extra for greasing

¼ cup **granulated sugar**

⅓ cup **all-purpose flour**

1 teaspoon **baking powder**

⅓ cup **shredded coconut**

1 **egg**

1 tablespoon **milk**

Preheat the slow cooker if necessary. Lightly grease 4 metal pudding basins, 1 cup each, and line the bottoms with nonstick parchment paper. Divide the corn syrup and brown sugar among them, then place three-quarters of the pineapple on top with the cherries.

Place the remaining pineapple with all the remaining ingredients into a mixing bowl and beat together until smooth. Spoon the batter into the pudding basins, level the surfaces with the back of a small spoon, then cover the tops with greased foil and put in the slow cooker pot.

Pour boiling water into the slow cooker pot to come halfway up the sides of the basins, cover, and cook on High for 2–2½ hours, until the sponge is well risen and springs back when pressed with a fingertip.

Remove the foil, loosen the edges of the puddings with a round-bladed knife and turn out into shallow bowls. Peel away the lining paper and serve.

For plum & almond puddings, follow the recipe above, using 4 pitted and sliced red plums instead of the pineapple and cherries. Omit the coconut and add ¼ cup ground almonds and a few drops of almond extract to the sponge batter instead. **Calories per serving 393**

232

gingered date & syrup puddings

Calories per serving **472**
Serves **4**
Preparation time **20 minutes**
Cooking time **3½–4 hours**

¾ cup **pitted dates**, chopped
½ cup boiling **water**
¼ teaspoon **baking soda**
4 tablespoons **sunflower margarine**, plus extra for greasing
¼ cup **light corn syrup**
¼ cup firmly packed **light brown sugar**
¾ cup **all-purpose flour**
¾ teaspoon **baking powder**
1 **egg**
1 teaspoon **vanilla extract**
1 teaspoon **ground ginger**
2 small scoops of **low-fat vanilla ice cream**

Preheat the slow cooker if necessary. Place the dates, boiling water, and baking soda in a bowl, stir, and set aside for 10 minutes.

Lightly grease 4 metal pudding basins, ¾ cup each, and line the bottoms with nonstick parchment paper. Divide the corn syrup among the basins.

Place the margarine, sugar, flour, egg, baking powder, vanilla, and ginger in a food processor and blend until smooth. Drain the dates, add to the processor and blend briefly to mix. Divide the batter among the pudding basins, cover the tops with greased foil and put in the slow cooker pot.

Pour boiling water into the slow cooker pot to come halfway up the sides of the basins, cover, and cook on High for 3½–4 hours until the sponge is well risen and springs back when pressed with a fingertip.

Remove the foil, loosen the edges of the puddings with a round-bladed knife, and turn out into shallow bowls. Peel away the lining paper and serve immediately with the ice cream.

For sticky banana puddings, omit the dates, boiling water, and baking soda. Follow the recipe above, adding 1 ripe banana to the food processor with the remaining ingredients. Blend and continue as above. **Calories per serving 411**

index

acknowledgments

Senior Commissioning Editor: Eleanor Maxfield
Editor: Pollyanna Poulter
Design: Jeremy Tilston & Jaz Bahra
Production Controller: Sarah Kramer
Photographer: William Shaw
Americanizer: Nicole Foster

Photography copyright © Octopus Publishing Group/ Stephen Conroy 6, 9, 10, 11, 13, 14, 15, 16, 27, 33, 35, 37, 39, 52, 55, 59, 69, 97, 99, 101, 103, 105, 147, 165, 167, 169, 171, 175, 209, 211, 213, 215, 217, 221, 223, 225, 227, 229, 233; Lis Parsons 118, 178; Ian Wallace 18.